MARTHA COLLISON

HarperCollins*Publishers*
1 London Bridge Street
London SE1 9GF
www.harpercollins.co.uk

First published by HarperCollins*Publishers* 2017

10 9 8 7 6 5 4 3 2 1

Text © Martha Collison 2017
Photography © Laura Edwards 2017
Illustration © Debbie Powell 2017

Martha Collison asserts the moral right to be identified as the author of this work

The Great British Bake Off Contestant logo™ is licensed by Love Productions Ltd

A catalogue record of this book is available from the British Library

ISBN 978-0-00-823863-6

Food styling: Annie Rigg
Prop styling: Polly Webb-Wilson

Printed and bound in China

MIX
Paper from
responsible sources
FSC™ C007454

FSC™ is a non-profit international organisation established to promote the responsible management of the world's forests. Products carrying the FSC label are independently certified to assure consumers that they come from forests that are managed to meet the social, economic and ecological needs of present and future generations, and other controlled sources.

Find out more about HarperCollins and the environment at
www.harpercollins.co.uk/green

Crave

Brilliantly indulgent recipes

MARTHA COLLISON

HarperCollins*Publishers*

Contents

Introduction

I have loved food for as long as I can remember. I was the child who looked forward to grocery shopping because I loved to see all the fresh fruits piled precariously in displays and to marvel at the number of intricately shaped pasta varieties in their colourful packets. Trailing slowly behind my mum, I'd wander through the aisles trying to sneak the new foods that I was curious to try into the trolley. I couldn't (and still can't) make it home with an intact baguette, as resisting the temptation to tear off the knobbly end and sink my teeth into the golden crust encasing the soft, chewy bread was beyond me. I'd spend Sunday afternoons thumbing through my mum's Nigella collection, devouring the pages with my eyes and picking out recipes to try to persuade my parents to let me make.

I was the girl who always had a hot school dinner because I hated the mundane predictability of a packed lunch. Taking my plastic tray up to the hatch and choosing a meal that I felt like eating was an experience to which I would look forward with great anticipation. The food may not have been incredible, but I had the choice of what I ate, and I loved it. In restaurants, I'd always ask for a spare plate rather than a meal of my own so I could sample everyone else's food at the table instead. I adored having a little taste of everything. I remember being sorely disappointed when I became too old for the empty-plate approach to be socially acceptable and had to order my own food. I couldn't relate to fussy eaters, as the thought of not knowing how a new food sitting on my plate tasted was an alien concept to me. I've been fascinated by flavour and had a thirst to understand food for longer than I've been able to cook it.

My earliest memory of a craving (embarrassing as this is for a baker who valiantly aims to champion homemade cooking) is butterscotch Angel Delight. I was transfixed by the kitchen magic that occurred; how whisking a beige powder with cold milk would transform it into a thick, cloudy mass with an unnatural, gelatinous texture. My sister and

I adored it, and the artificial buttery flavour evokes a certain nostalgia that I've struggled to replicate. We crave the things we love; the foods that make us happy. That's how the idea for this book was born.

Crave is a book focused on my love affair with food; on glorifying ingredients in their purest form as well as showing how to combine flavours to create sensational bakes. Living in an age crammed full of dieting and healthy-eating cookbooks, I was desperate for a change, and I hope *Crave* offers just that. This is a book that should speak to that inner voice we all have which asks 'What do I really feel like eating?' It is aimed squarely at loving, appreciating and celebrating food for what it is, without an ounce of guilt for indulging the body and mind in what they desire. By no means am I suggesting that you throw healthy eating out of the window and base your diet on these recipes; I am fully supportive of eating a balanced, nutritious diet. However, I am also a firm believer in the importance of treating yourself every now and again. Food, especially baking, should be fun! This book is full of recipes that will satisfy your cravings on those self-indulgent days.

Cravings are a curious phenomenon. What starts as an insignificant little niggle at the back of your mind, gently hinting at the kind of food needed to hit the spot, can quickly grow into a compulsion that demands to be satisfied. The kind that drives you out of bed in the middle of the night to raid the fridge for a morsel of cheese, or causes you to sneak away from your desk in a desperate hunt for a square of chocolate to go with your coffee. This book is organised into chapters focused on eight of the most common cravings: Citrus, Fruit, Nut, Spice, Chocolate, Caramel, Cheese and Alcohol. Starting with recipes for refreshing citrus breakfasts to start the day with vigour, through ambrosial caramel delights to satisfy even the sweetest tooth, and ending with dark and devious ways to imbue delectable bakes with alcoholic tipples, there is something here to sate every appetite.

In the words of Virginia Woolf:

'One cannot think well, love well, sleep well, if one has not dined well.'

Crave is everything I love about baking. I bake to please, to nurture, to comfort, to entertain and, most importantly, to enjoy, and I hope that radiates through these pages.

How to use this book

I bake with immediate consumption in mind. I'm an impatient baker, and I want to be rewarded for my toils as quickly as possible – whether that is with a super-quick bake or by sneaking a spoonful of hot gooey brownies fresh from the oven before they have had the chance to cool. The three categories of recipes represent the different amounts of time needed to create bakes to satisfy your cravings. You'll notice the headers at the top of each recipe page.

INSTANT

These recipes take less than 20 minutes. They are go-to quick treats that can be rustled up in next to no time when you need something to hit the spot. You'll find clever tips and shortcuts to help speed up your favourite bakes.

SOON

Taking less than an hour to create from start to finish, these include everything from amazingly quick cakes to biscuits and savoury snacks. These are the recipes that you can always sneak a bite from while they cool, if you can't wait any longer.

WORTH THE WAIT

These recipes take over an hour, allowing plenty of time for more lengthy baking processes, such as proving and rising, and for flavours to steep right into bakes. These are recipes that truly reward the patience you expend and will not disappoint you.

The key to fitting these recipes into the allotted time is preparation. Set out and measure all your ingredients before you begin so you don't waste time scouring the kitchen for a missing item or get halfway through and realise you've run out of something vital. Do the same with your equipment, so that once you are in the swing of things, everything is within easy reach. Remember to preheat the oven before you start, too. I have timed and tested these recipes vigilantly to make sure they are achievable in the time specified. Some might take a little practice at first, but your go-to recipes will soon become second nature.

Some flavours are perfect partners and it's a regular occurrence for me to find myself craving not one but two (or even more!) flavours and ingredients – dark chocolate and orange, warming spices and caramel, or savoury cheese with sweet fruit. I've flagged these classic combos with small icons on the recipe pages.

Citrus | Fruit | Nut | Spice | Chocolate | Caramel | Cheese | Alcohol

Equipment

My kitchen is bursting at the seams with equipment, some that I use every single day and couldn't bear to be without, and some that sits gathering dust for most of the year. This is a list of my essential kit, the things I use on a regular basis that aid my baking.

Electric mixers

Electric hand-held whisks and stand mixers are a godsend. They make cake making so much quicker, and are essential for tasks like whipping egg whites and making light buttercreams. Electric hand-held whisks are more affordable than stand mixers, but if you bake a lot, a stand mixer such as a KitchenAid or Kenwood kMix is a worthwhile investment: it will revolutionise the way you bake.

Wire cooling racks

Often overlooked, wire racks are really important in making sure whatever you've put time and effort into baking yields the very best results. Elevating a hot bake allows air to circulate and prevents condensation from forming, avoiding sogginess and helping the bake cool evenly and quickly.

Baking tins

Perhaps the most essential kit. They come in all shapes and sizes, so it can be daunting choosing which ones to invest in. The tins I regularly use and recommend purchasing are round 18cm and 20cm deep loose-bottomed tins, ideally three of each so you don't have to bake in batches for a multi-layered cake. A 20 x 20cm square tin, 450g loaf tin, 12-hole muffin tin, 24-hole mini muffin tin, pie dish and a 20 x 35cm traybake tin are also useful.

Baking trays and baking sheets

Although they are very similar, baking trays and sheets serve different purposes so I have both in my kitchen. Baking trays have a lip around the edge to prevent whatever you're baking rolling off the edge (ideal for roasting nuts). Baking sheets are completely flat, so there is more surface area to bake cookies or biscuits.

Jars, bags and boxes

I always have an array of glass jars, presentation bags and cake boxes on hand so that anything I bake can be easily packaged as a gift. Jars need sterilising before you fill them. To do this, simply wash them thoroughly in hot soapy water, rinse with clean water then dry them completely in an oven preheated to 110°C/90°C fan/gas ¼ (this will take 5–10 minutes) before filling.

Food processors

These are handy for both sweet and savoury cooking. They cut the time it takes to chop nuts and create purées, and can even make pastry without you getting your hands dirty. Powerful processors are expensive, so for a more budget-friendly option, go for a mini food processor or stick blender with a chopping bowl attachment, which are perfect for blitzing small quantities of nuts, dough or praline for 'instant' recipes.

Ice-cream scoops

I use ice-cream scoops for so much more than scooping ice-cream. In fact, it is probably one of my most-used pieces of kitchen equipment. I have three sizes and they are ideal for making even-sized cupcakes, perfectly circular cookies and distributing batters between cake tins.

Palette knives

To get a beautiful, smooth finish on iced cakes, you will need a palette knife. I have a larger one for smoothing the edges of my cakes, and a mini offset knife for adding detail to the top of cakes.

Piping bags and nozzles

I use disposable piping bags as they're so handy – you can snip off the end of the bags once filled, creating holes of various sizes without always needing to use a nozzle. Where I suggest a disposable bag, do use a reusable piping bag if you prefer. For icing cupcakes and large cakes, my favourite nozzles are open and closed stars, as they create a beautiful ruffled effect.

Baking parchment and baking sheet liners

I find lining tins time-consuming and a real chore, so I buy pre-cut circles of baking parchment the same sizes as my round tins. They reduce preparation time and are ideal for my 'Instant' and 'Soon' recipes. I cover baking sheets with a reusable non-stick baking liner to save the need to grease them.

Digital scales

Reliable, good-quality digital scales are a must. Baking is a science that requires accuracy to obtain good results, so inaccurate scales will limit you.

Measuring spoons

A common measurement people get wrong is teaspoon and tablespoon measures, as it is very easy to overestimate or underestimate spoon measures if you're weighing by eye or using ordinary cutlery. Get hold of a cook's measuring spoon set.

Ingredients

Fresh, good-quality ingredients raise an average bake to a great one and really make it sing. These are my top storecupboard ingredients which I make sure I always have in stock.

Eggs

The humble egg is the most versatile ingredient in baking. It can be used to bind mixtures, aerate puddings, thicken custards and set into firm structures like meringue. I use medium free-range eggs in my recipes unless otherwise stated. Fresh eggs yield the lightest, fluffiest bakes, so use your freshest eggs for making cake batters. Slightly older eggs will make brilliant meringues or macarons. Store your eggs at room temperature for baking – egg whites and yolks combine much more easily at room temperature and will disperse through batter more smoothly.

Butter

Butter is my favourite ingredient by far to use in baking. Its rich, full flavour is what makes caramels so moreish and ganache so smooth. I always use salted butter in baking unless otherwise specified. I find the saltiness is the perfect partner for sweet and savoury recipes and it's what I spread liberally on my toast, so its something I always have to hand. Unsalted butter is necessary in some cases – buttercreams and delicate pastries can be overwhelmed by salt, so keep this in mind. Use the butter at the temperature that the recipe states – cold for pastry and room temperature for sponge or buttercream – as this can make or break a bake.

Milk

Many chefs specify whole milk for baking, but if you don't normally have it in the fridge, don't buy it especially unless the recipe specifies it. Whole milk has a high percentage of butterfat (a minimum of 3.5%) so can yield a creamier result, but semi-skimmed milk (1.5–1.8% butterfat) will still do the job. I often use semi-skimmed milk to make bakes, and it works perfectly.

Raising agents

Baking powder and bicarbonate of soda are the two raising agents I use to make bakes rise or spread out. For any chemistry geeks like me who want to know how they work, here's a brief explanation. A reaction between an acid and a base creates carbon dioxide bubbles, which cause a cake mixture to rise. Bicarbonate of soda is a base, so an acidic ingredient needs to be present in the mixture for it to react with to create the bubbles. Lemon juice, buttermilk or cocoa powder, among many others, do the trick. Baking powder is a combination of bicarbonate of soda (a base) and cream of tartar (an acid), so both the acid and base required for the reaction are already present, and your bake will rise with no further assistance.

Salt

There are many different kinds of salt available, so it can be confusing to know what's best for baking. Fine table salt is generally what's called for, as its fine texture can evenly disperse throughout bread dough and cake batter. Sea salt has a better flavour and is perfect for adding a final flourish to caramels, breads and snacks.

Sugar

From clouds of white icing sugar to clumps of moist, fudgy, soft, dark brown sugar, there are so many varieties of the sweet stuff that, when used in baking, produce completely different results. Caster sugar is the most commonly used in this book as its fine texture and neutral flavour provide a great base for most sweet recipes. I try to buy Fairtrade sugar to ensure that it is grown and harvested ethically (it is rarely pricier than standard sugar).

Yeast

I use fast-action dried yeast (also known as instant, easy-blend or easy-bake yeast) in baking as I find it the easiest to work with. It doesn't need to be activated with warm water or milk, it can just be added straight to dry ingredients and will work perfectly. Always check the use-by date on packs of yeast, as out-of-date yeast may fail to make your bread rise.

Flour

I use a mixture of self-raising flour and plain flour in this book, as I always seem to have a glut of both flours, and it seems a shame to let one go to waste. If a recipe specifies self-raising flour but you don't have any, you can easily substitute it by adding ½ a teaspoon of baking powder to 100g plain flour and using this in its place. Strong bread flour is essential in bread-making and some pastries as it contains a higher level of gluten necessary for maintaining structure.

Citrus

Understanding *Citrus*

Nothing awakens a half-asleep body like a morning sip of sharp orange juice or soothes illness like warmed lemon and honey. A glass of ice-cold lemonade is all you need to feel summery, and an afternoon making marmalade in the Seville orange season in January and February is a midwinter ray of sunshine.

My grandma starts her day with half a grapefruit, cutting into it with a spoon and bursting through the segments, creating a spray of juice that showers everyone at the table. I once thought I could handle it, but the tart, tangy flavour was overwhelming for my young taste buds. I've since learnt that citrus juice can be variously mellowed, perhaps adding sugar to make drizzles for cakes or incorporating it into creamy cheesecakes or possets.

Slicing into citrus fruits reveals a complex network of brightly coloured, almost translucent segments packed with tiny juice sacs that glisten in the light. They are held together by geometrically satisfying strips of white pith, which allow the fruits to fall apart neatly when peeled and split into segments.

When selecting citrus fruits for baking, choose firm, brightly coloured specimens that feel heavy for their size, as they should yield the most juice. If you are going to grate or pare the zest (which I recommend, as it contains the citrus oils that characterise each fruit), be sure to buy them unwaxed, as the protective wax coating applied to fruits has a bitter flavour and tough texture. If you can't find unwaxed fruits, remove the wax by washing them in hot water and scrubbing them with a brush. Before juicing fruits, roll them on a worktop. The pressure of rolling bursts open some of the segments inside, which makes them easier to juice.

Tenderising

Citrus juices, when mixed into cake batters, can act as a tenderiser, making for a lighter, softer sponge. The added acids interfere with gluten formation, which prevents the cake becoming tough and chewy as the gluten network is not as strong. *See*: Lemon and Lime Battenberg

Acidity

A simple acid and alkali reaction happens when citric acid found in citrus fruits comes into contact with bicarbonate of soda or baking powder. They react and produce carbon dioxide bubbles which make bakes rise. This reaction happens as soon as they are mixed together, so don't leave batter standing around for long or you'll find your bakes won't rise well. *See*: Lemon and Poppy Seed Pancake Stack

Preserving

When the acid in citrus juice makes contact with the cut flesh of certain fruits (such as apples, pears or bananas) it reacts with oxygen to stop the fruits going brown. If you're slicing fruit for a bake, squeeze half a lemon into a bowl of water and submerge the fruit until ready to use, to stop them browning. *See*: Sweet and Sour Apple Crisps

Thickening

If you add lemon juice to milk to make buttermilk and leave it long enough, it curdles. This acidified milk generates rise when used with raising agents and adds a tangy flavour to cakes. Citrus juice can also act as a thickener when added to cream, as the balance of protein and fat prevents curdling but yields a smooth thickness which creates a creamy texture, making it ideal for desserts. *See*: Grapefruit and White Chocolate Posset

Limoncello brandy snap curls

Once you try making your own brandy snaps, they will no longer be condemned to the folder marked 'difficult bakes'. These delicious retro treats are made with storecupboard ingredients and can be whipped up quickly if you make a small quantity. The key here is to be vigilant when you're weighing the ingredients; being a few grams out really does make a difference in this recipe. I've paired the snaps with a limoncello cream because I love the way it brings out the citrus flavour in the brandy snap, but if you'd rather make alcohol-free brandy snaps substitute the limoncello for lemon juice or just dip them into plain whipped cream.

MAKES 8 BRANDY
SNAP CURLS

PREP TIME: 10 MINS
PLUS COOLING

COOKING TIME:
6–8 MINS

Oil, for greasing
25g butter
25g soft light brown sugar
25g golden syrup
Grated zest of 1 unwaxed
    lemon and 1 tsp juice
25g plain flour

LIMONCELLO CREAM
100ml double cream
1 tsp icing sugar
1 tbsp limoncello

1. Preheat the oven to 180°C/160°C fan/gas 4, line 2 baking trays with baking parchment and grease a rolling pin or long, thin bottle with oil.

2. Stir the butter, sugar and golden syrup together in a small saucepan over a medium heat until the butter has melted and the sugar has dissolved. Remove the pan from the heat and stir in the lemon juice and zest, reserving a pinch to garnish the limoncello cream.

3. Sift the flour into the saucepan and beat it into the mixture until a smooth dough forms.

4. Using a teaspoon, drop about 4 heaps of mixture on to each tray. It will be fairly runny, but this is normal. Make sure that you leave space between the heaps, as they will spread out when they bake.

5. Bake for 6–8 minutes until golden brown, spread out and bubbly. Remove from the oven and allow them to cool for a minute so they mould easily without tearing. As they cool they take on their signature lacy pattern.

6. Wedge the greased rolling pin or bottle between a couple of heavy objects so it is stable when you place the snaps on it. Use a palette knife to lift the warm snaps on to the rolling pin and gently press them down so they bend around the cylinder to make curls. Leave to set until cool and crisp.

7. Whisk the cream, icing sugar and limoncello in a bowl until the mixture forms soft peaks then spoon it into a small serving bowl. Top with the reserved lemon zest. Use the brandy snap curls to scoop the lemon cream as a treat to share or as a dessert.

Lemon and pistachio cheesecake pots

No-bake cheesecakes are one of my guilty pleasures. I used to make these pots for my sister and me when we were young, and she'd always be in awe of how quickly I could create a cheesecake. We'd try different flavours, depending on what we had in the cupboard, but this is my favourite: creamy lemon and vibrant green pistachios with a layer of luscious lemon curd peeking through in the centre. Try this recipe with any combination of curd or nuts to tailor it to any fussy family member!

1. To make the base, melt the butter in the microwave or in a small saucepan. Place the digestive biscuits in a small food processor with the pistachios and blitz until the biscuits and the nuts are crushed. If you haven't got a food processor, crush the biscuits to a powder by putting them in a bag and bashing them with a rolling pin. Finely chop the nuts with a sharp knife and combine them with the crushed biscuits. Place the ground biscuits and nuts in a bowl and stir in the melted butter. Divide the mixture between 2 small glasses and press it down into an even layer. Transfer to the fridge to chill.

2. Beat the cream cheese for the filling with the lemon juice and icing sugar in a small bowl until smooth. Stir through half the lemon zest, reserving the rest for decoration.

3. Divide half the cream cheese mixture between the biscuit bases, then top with the lemon curd. Finish with the rest of the cream cheese mixture. Top with the rest of the lemon zest and a few chopped pistachio nuts. You can eat these desserts straight away or make up to 3 days ahead and keep them in the fridge.

MAKES 2 CHEESECAKE POTS

PREP TIME: 15 MINS PLUS CHILLING TIME

COOKING TIME: 2 MINS

BASE
25g butter
60g digestive biscuits
40g pistachio nuts, plus extra to decorate

FILLING
200g full-fat cream cheese
Grated zest and juice of ½ unwaxed lemon
2 tbsp icing sugar
2 tbsp lemon curd

Coconut and lime teacup puddings

This is a sophisticated, tea-party twist on a mug cake. The liquid poured over the top serves two purposes: it keeps the sponge moist, which is really important in a microwaved sponge as they have a tendency to dry out, and it soaks through the pudding, creating a surprise citrus sauce at the bottom of the cup.

MAKES 2 PUDDINGS

PREP TIME: 5 MINS

COOKING TIME: 2 MINS IN THE MICROWAVE OR 12–14 MINS IN THE OVEN

50g butter, plus extra for greasing
50g self-raising flour
50g caster sugar
1 egg
Grated zest and juice of ½ unwaxed lime
25ml coconut milk from a shaken can
25g granulated sugar

1. Grease 2 oven-safe porcelain teacups or ramekins with plenty of butter and set to one side.

2. In a small food processor, blitz the butter, flour, caster sugar and egg together until they resemble a smooth, thick batter. (You can do this by hand in a large bowl, but it will take a little longer.) Fold through the lime zest and divide the mixture between the 2 teacups or ramekins.

3. Mix together the coconut milk, lime juice and granulated sugar in a small jug. Pour this mixture over the puddings so the top is covered in liquid.

4. Cook in the microwave on full power for 2 minutes until the cake is risen and the top is springy. Alternatively, bake in an oven preheated to 200°C/180°C fan/gas 6 for 12–14 minutes until they are risen and golden.

5. Allow to cool for a minute or two before turning out on to a plate or enjoying straight from the cup or ramekin.

Caramelised marmalade French toast

Perennially popular French toast is a fantastically fast and impressive-looking breakfast dish. It's a great way to use up slices of leftover bread, too – I use brioche here for its rich, sweet flavour but any type of bread will work. This is my favourite way to eat French toast: sticky and caramelised in the marmalade, with an oozing melted chocolate centre. Bitter orange with rich chocolate and sweet brioche is a combination to die for.

SERVES 2

PREP TIME: 5 MINS

COOKING TIME:
10 MINS

1 egg
125ml whole milk
1 tsp vanilla extract
Grated zest of 1 unwaxed
   orange and juice of ½
25g caster sugar
¼ x 400g brioche loaf
2 tbsp dark chocolate
   chips
25g butter
2 tbsp orange marmalade

1. Beat together the egg, milk, vanilla extract and orange zest in a wide dish that is large enough to accommodate a slice of brioche comfortably. Add the sugar to the mix and beat again.

2. Cut 2 thick slices from the brioche loaf and slice each piece diagonally in half to make 4 triangles. Make a small horizontal incision in the side of each slice using a sharp knife and stuff the cavity with a few chocolate chips, then pinch the edges together to seal.

3. Melt the butter in a large frying pan or griddle pan over a medium–high heat. Dip each stuffed slice of brioche into the egg mixture and allow to soak briefly until saturated. Fry each slice until browned and caramelised on the bottom, then flip over and cook for a further 1–2 minutes on the other side. Remove from the pan and keep warm while you fry the remaining pieces.

4. Heat the marmalade and orange juice together in the frying pan until bubbling. Allow to bubble for 1–2 minutes, then return the French toast slices to the pan with the marmalade and coat them in the glaze. Serve immediately.

Lime and ginger drizzle cake traybake

Changing the type of drizzle on a cake is now commonplace, but don't forget that you can change the cake, too – don't just stick to vanilla sponge! Ginger cake is already deliciously moist, but drenching it in lime juice mixed with demerara sugar only improves it further. Citrus flavours like lemon or lime lighten warm spices like ginger and make each square of this cake really refreshing.

1. Preheat the oven to 180°C/160°C fan/gas 4, grease the cake tin and line it with baking parchment.

2. Place the butter, sugar, treacle and syrup in a large saucepan over a medium heat and stir continuously until the butter has melted and the sugar has completely dissolved.

3. Remove from the heat and pour the milk into the saucepan of hot butter and sugar mixture, whisking until combined. This will cool the mixture down before you add the egg, preventing it from scrambling. Beat the eggs into the mixture one at a time, then stir in the chopped stem ginger and most of the lime zest, reserving some for decoration.

4. Mix together the flour, bicarbonate of soda and ground ginger in a large bowl. Sift the dry ingredients into the wet ingredients in the saucepan and beat until well combined.

5. Pour the batter into the lined tin and bake in the middle of the oven for 30–35 minutes or until risen and a skewer inserted into the centre comes out clean.

6. While the cake is baking, prepare the drizzle. Mix the lime juice and demerara sugar together in a small jug. Just 5 minutes after the cake comes out of the oven, while it's still in the tin, pour over the drizzle and spread it right to the edges of the cake. Sprinkle over the crystallised ginger cubes (if using) and remaining lime zest, then leave to stand for at least 15 minutes so the drizzle can soak into the sponge properly. Remove from the tin and cut the cake into squares. This cake will keep for up to 1 week.

MAKES ABOUT 16 SQUARES

PREP TIME: 15 MINS PLUS COOLING

COOKING TIME: 30–35 MINS

200g butter, plus extra for greasing
250g soft dark brown sugar
50g treacle
100g golden syrup
100ml milk
2 eggs
1 ball stem ginger from a jar in syrup, finely chopped
Grated zest of 1 unwaxed lime
250g plain flour
1 tsp bicarbonate of soda
1 tsp ground ginger

DRIZZLE
Juice of 3 limes
100g demerara sugar
25g crystallised ginger, cut into small cubes (optional)

You will also need a 20 x 20cm cake tin.

Lemon and poppy seed pancake stack

This is lazy weekend food, for those times when towering stacks of fluffy pancakes dripping in syrup are the only thing worth crawling out from under the duvet for. The lemon juice in the batter serves two functions: it gives the pancakes a beautiful flavour, and its acidity reacts with bicarbonate of soda to make them rise up into soft pillows.

1. In a small bowl, mix together the flour, bicarbonate of soda, baking powder and sugar. Beat together the egg, milk and yoghurt in a large jug, then pour the wet ingredients into the dry ingredients and stir until just combined. Stir in the lemon juice, zest and poppy seeds.

2. Melt the butter in a large frying pan over a medium heat, then add it to the pancake batter and mix until smooth.

3. When you're ready to fry the pancakes, use an ice-cream scoop or simply transfer the batter back into the jug and pour roughly 8cm-diameter discs into the buttered frying pan. Try to make each pancake the same size, so they stack neatly on top of each other. Fry each pancake for about 1 minute on each side over a medium heat, waiting until the top of the pancake is bubbly but feels dry before turning it. Add a very small amount of butter between frying each one if the pancakes start to stick. Put the cooked pancakes on a baking tray in a low oven, covered with a sheet of tin foil, so you can serve all the pancakes warm at the same time.

4. While the pancakes are frying, make the lemon syrup. Place the caster sugar and lemon juice in a small saucepan over a low heat and let it boil until the sugar dissolves. When the syrup is thick and bubbling, stir in the butter and double cream.

5. Stack the pancakes up on a plate, then pour the syrup over the top of the pancakes so it drips down the sides. Top with a little whipped cream or a spoonful of mascarpone cheese, then serve immediately.

EXPRESS

Make the pancake batter in advance and store it in the fridge, covered with a sheet of cling film. Fry the pancakes whenever you get a craving for something light, fluffy and citrusy! The batter will keep for up to 3 days.

MAKES 8 PANCAKES

PREP TIME: 10 MINS

COOKING TIME: 15–20 MINS

150g plain flour
½ tsp bicarbonate of soda
½ tsp baking powder
1 tbsp caster sugar
1 egg
100ml milk
100g natural yoghurt
Grated zest and juice of 1 unwaxed lemon
1 tbsp poppy seeds
25g butter, plus extra for frying (if needed)
Whipped cream or mascarpone cheese, to serve

LEMON SYRUP
100g caster sugar
Juice of 1 lemon
Small knob of butter
1 tbsp double cream

Orange, pistachio and pomegranate cakes

Combining fruits with nuts in baking is a timeless, tried-and-tested combination that you can rarely go wrong with. I've added citrus to the mix in the form of partially caramelised juicy orange, which adds another dimension to the cakes. Glossy, colourful fruit sits proudly on top of a moist pistachio cake, and the syrup created from the fruit and sugar soaks into the sponge, making these cakes incredibly moreish.

1. Preheat the oven to 180°C/160°C fan/gas 4 and grease the muffin tin with butter. Divide 45g of the caster sugar between 9 of the holes (a teaspoon/5g in each).

2. Use a sharp knife to cut the top and bottom off each orange, then slice off the skin, keeping as much of the flesh intact as possible. Slice the oranges into cross sections, then quarter each section and place two segments into each hole of the tin opposite each other, with the curved edge sitting against the sides. Fill the remaining quarters of each hole with a layer of pomegranate seeds. Bake the fruit in the oven for 10 minutes so they start to caramelise.

3. Blitz the pistachio nuts in a food processor until they resemble a fine powder. Cream together the butter and remaining sugar in a separate bowl until light and fluffy, then beat in the eggs one at a time. Add the flour, baking powder and ground pistachios to the bowl and continue to beat until the mixture is smooth.

4. When the fruit has baked for 10 minutes, remove the tin from the oven. Divide the cake batter among each hole, spreading it right to the edges, and bake for 20–25 minutes or until the cakes are risen and a skewer inserted into the centre of one of the cakes comes out clean.

5. Leave the cakes to cool in the tin for a few minutes, then run a knife or palette knife around the edge of each cake to make them easier to remove, then turn the whole tray out upside down over a board. A bit of hot syrup might escape as you turn the tray, so be very careful. Serve the cakes hot, with a big scoop of ice-cream, or cold with a cup of hot coffee.

MAKES 9 CAKES

PREP TIME: 20 MINS

COOKING TIME: 30–35 MINS

170g caster sugar
2 medium oranges
Seeds from ½ pomegranate
75g unshelled pistachio nuts, shelled
125g butter, softened, plus extra for greasing
2 eggs
50g plain flour
½ tsp baking powder

You will also need a 12-hole muffin tin.

Grapefruit and white chocolate possets with shortbread

The science behind posset is fascinating. When you add acidic lemon juice to milk, it curdles, but cream's higher fat percentage limits its ability to follow suit. Instead, the acidified cream thickens and becomes silky and smooth. I add white chocolate to my posset as its creamy sweetness really lifts the sharp yet fragrant grapefruit to a new level.

MAKES 6 POSSETS AND 10–12 BISCUITS

PREP TIME: 15 MINS PLUS CHILLING

COOKING TIME: 20–22 MINS

500ml double cream
150g caster sugar
100g white chocolate, chopped
Juice of ½ lemon
Grated zest and juice of 1 small unwaxed pink grapefruit
Icing sugar, white chocolate curls and grapefruit zest, to decorate

GRAPEFRUIT SHORTBREAD
115g plain flour
35g caster sugar
75g cold butter, cubed
Grated zest of 1 small unwaxed pink grapefruit

1. Pop 6 shallow glasses into the freezer to chill. You can use any style of glass for this recipe, but the deeper the glasses, the longer the posset will take to set.

2. Pour the cream into a large heavy-based saucepan and add the sugar. Heat over a low heat, stirring, until the grains of sugar have dissolved, then turn up the heat and boil for 2 minutes, stirring constantly. The boiling cream will double or triple in size, so make sure you've chosen a large enough saucepan. Remove from the heat and stir in the chopped white chocolate.

3. Keep stirring until no lumps of chocolate remain, then pour in the lemon juice and the zest and juice of the grapefruit, and mix thoroughly. The mixture will thicken as the acid is added to the milk.

4. Pour the posset mixture into the chilled glasses and place the glasses in the freezer for 45 minutes to set, then enjoy immediately or transfer to the fridge until you're ready to serve. If you're making these ahead of time you can keep them in the fridge without using the freezer, where they will take around 3 hours to set. Dust the top of the set possets with icing sugar then decorate with white chocolate curls and grapefruit zest.

5. While the possets are chilling, make the shortbread. Preheat the oven to 200°C/180°C fan/gas 6 and line a baking tray with baking parchment. Place the flour, caster sugar and butter in a food processor and pulse until the mixture begins to clump together, then add the grapefruit zest. You could do this in a large bowl and use your fingers to rub the butter into the flour. Tip out on to a large sheet of cling film, then roll into a log and freeze for at least 15 minutes.

6. Unwrap the dough and slice into 10–12 rounds using a sharp knife. Arrange on the lined baking tray and bake for 10–12 minutes, until a pale golden brown. Remove from the oven and then leave to cool completely. Serve the shortbread with the chilled, set possets.

Lemonade marshmallows

There is nothing better than relaxing with a refreshing glass of homemade cloudy lemonade on a warm summer's day, and these little marshmallow bites recreate that holiday feeling. You can adapt this recipe to suit your taste by using any kind of drink as the base for the marshmallow. Pink lemonade or cream soda work especially well or try champagne for a special occasion. They make great gifts.

MAKES 25 LARGE SQUARES

PREP TIME: 30 MINS PLUS SETTING TIME

Oil, for greasing
125ml cloudy lemonade
Grated zest and juice of
½ unwaxed lemon
2 x 12g sachets gelatine
powder
450g caster sugar
150g golden syrup
100g icing sugar
2 tbsp cornflour

You will also need a sugar thermometer

1. Line a baking tray with oiled cling film and set to one side.

2. Pour the lemonade and lemon juice into a large bowl or the bowl of a stand mixer, and sprinkle over the gelatine powder. Set aside to allow the gelatine to absorb all the liquid.

3. While the gelatine is soaking, put the caster sugar and golden syrup in a saucepan with enough water to cover (around 150ml). Cook over a low heat, stirring all the time, until the sugar has dissolved. As soon as there are no visible grains of sugar, stop stirring, turn up the heat and bring the mixture to the boil. Place a sugar thermometer in the pan and once it reads 130°C take the pan off the heat and allow to cool for 1 minute until the mixture is no longer bubbling.

4. Start whisking the gelatine and lemonade mixture with an electric hand-held whisk or in a stand mixer on a medium speed. Add the syrup mixture, slowly pouring it down the side of the bowl, whisking all the time. Try to avoid pouring it directly on to the whisk or you will get grainy lumps of sugar in the marshmallow. After a few minutes, the mixture should become pale and grow in volume like a very stiff meringue.

5. Once all the syrup has been added, continue to whisk for 5–10 minutes, until the marshmallow mixture becomes really thick. The mixture is ready when the outside of the bowl feels just slightly warm and the marshmallow is starting to get really sticky.

6. Use an oiled spatula to spread the mixture into the lined baking tray, then leave it to set for 2–3 hours at room temperature or until the marshmallow feels firm. Sift the icing sugar and cornflour together into a bowl and stir through the lemon zest. Turn the marshmallow out of the tin, peel off the cling film, then dust the whole marshmallow slab with the powder. Cut into small cubes using a sharp, oiled knife. The marshmallows will keep for 1–2 weeks in an airtight container.

Lemon meringue profiteroles

This is my take on a lemon meringue pie – choux-style! Deliciously light pastry stuffed with zingy lemon cream, entirely enrobed in Italian meringue. Whenever my family hosts a spontaneous dinner party or family lunch, profiteroles are one of my go-to recipes. You can replace the lemon curd with any kind of curd – lime, orange or passionfruit all work really well.

1. Preheat the oven to 180°C/160°C fan/gas 4 and line 2 large baking sheets with baking parchment.

2. To make the pastry, place the butter, sugar and 125ml of water in a small saucepan over a medium–high heat. Bring the mixture to a rolling boil, and when all the butter has melted add the flours and vigorously beat the mixture with a wooden spoon until a smooth ball of dough forms.

3. Keep the pan on the heat and continue to cook the dough, stirring rapidly, for a further minute. Tip the dough into a bowl and leave it to cool until it has stopped steaming, to avoid scrambling the eggs.

4. Beat the eggs together briefly in a small jug. Add the eggs to the cooled dough in three separate additions, beating well between each one with a wooden spoon or spatula, mixing until it turns into a thick paste. You might not need to add all the egg so when you are adding the final amount, add it slowly. Your mixture should fall off the spoon or spatula easily and leave a 'V' shape. Spoon the choux pastry into one of the piping bags.

5. Snip the end off the piping bag and pipe the dough into about thirty 2.5cm balls on the baking sheets, leaving enough space for them to spread out. Use a wet finger to smooth over any peaks. Bake for 20–25 minutes or until risen, golden brown and hollow, then turn off the oven and leave them in the oven (with the door closed) to cool completely. This will dry out the pastry.

6. While the pastry is drying, make the lemon cream filling. Whip the cream in a large bowl until it forms soft peaks, then fold it through the lemon curd and lemon zest. Spoon the mixture into a piping bag, and set it to one side.

7. To make the meringue topping, put the sugar in a small saucepan with 75ml of water over a medium heat and stir until the grains of sugar have dissolved, then bring the mixture to the boil and put a sugar thermometer in the pan.

MAKES ABOUT
30 PROFITEROLES

PREP TIME: 45–50 MINS
PLUS COOLING

COOKING TIME:
20–25 MINS

PASTRY
75g butter, diced
1 tsp caster sugar
50g plain flour
50g strong bread flour
3 eggs

LEMON CREAM FILLING
250ml double cream
100g lemon curd, plus
    2 tbsp for drizzling
Grated zest of 1 unwaxed
    lemon

ITALIAN MERINGUE
TOPPING
150g caster sugar
2 egg whites

You will also need three disposable piping bags, a sugar thermometer and a blowtorch.

8. While the syrup is heating up, whisk the egg whites in a clean, grease-free bowl using an electric hand-held whisk or a stand mixer until they form soft peaks.

9. When the sugar syrup reaches 118°C, pour it gradually down the side of the bowl into the whites, whisking all the time. Try to avoid pouring the syrup on to the beaters, as this will create hard sugar crystals. Continue to whisk the meringue for 10 minutes until it is really thick and glossy. Spoon the meringue mixture into the third piping bag so it is ready to use.

10. Pierce a small hole in the bottom of each cooled profiterole, snip the end off the lemon-cream piping bag and fill the profiteroles with the lemon cream. Arrange about 10 profiteroles on a large serving plate as the bottom layer. Construct a pyramid, using a little meringue as glue.

11. Pipe the meringue mixture around the profiterole stack. Use a blowtorch to brown the meringue to get the full lemon-meringue effect! Drizzle lemon curd over the top of the stack as a finishing touch.

Preserved lemon and olive focaccia

Preserved lemons originate from North Africa and have recently grown in popularity here in the UK. Soaking lemons in salt water doesn't sound like a radical concept, but it utterly transforms the often harsh flavour of lemon into something much mellower. You can bite straight into a slice of preserved lemon without any of that jaw-clenching sharpness, which allows you to enjoy the aromas and textures of lemon in a new way. I also use lemon-infused oil, which you can buy from good supermarkets, as the main oil in this dough, which disperses a gentle lemon flavour throughout.

MAKES 1 LOAF

PREP TIME: 30 MINS
PLUS PROVING TIME

COOKING TIME:
20 MINS

500g strong plain flour, plus extra for dusting
1 x 7g sachet fast-action dried yeast
2 tsp fine salt
30ml lemon-infused oil (or olive oil), plus extra olive oil for greasing
300ml lukewarm water
2–3 preserved lemons
100g pitted green and black olives
Sprig of fresh thyme, leaves stripped
Sea salt, for sprinkling

1. Place the flour in a large bowl or the bowl of a stand mixer fitted with the dough-hook attachment and add the yeast to one side of the bowl and the salt to the other. If you put the salt directly on the yeast it may kill it, which will stop your dough from rising.

2. Add the oil and 225ml of the water to the flour and stir the ingredients together using your hands or the dough-hook attachment until a rough dough forms. Gradually add the remaining water. The dough will be very wet, but don't worry – this is what creates the irregular holes in a focaccia.

3. Liberally grease your worktop with oil and turn the dough out on to it (or leave it in the stand mixer, if using). Knead for about 10 minutes, in the mixer or by hand, oiling your hands and the surfaces as necessary, until the dough is really smooth and stretchy. I find that using a dough scraper helps stop the dough sticking to the worktop. When you pull the dough apart, the strands should stretch, not break. Grease the bowl with oil and place the dough back into it (if you were kneading it on the worktop), cover with clingfilm and leave to rise at room temperature for 1–3 hours until doubled in size.

4. While the dough is rising, thinly slice the preserved lemons and set aside. Generously grease a baking tray with olive oil.

5. Carefully remove the dough from the bowl and turn it out on to a lightly floured worktop. You don't want to handle the dough too much, so don't knead it, just stretch it out to a large rectangle, then place it on the baking tray. Spread it right to the edges and use your fingers to make indentations over the surface of the dough.

6. Press the olives into some of the indentations and arrange the preserved lemon slices and thyme leaves on the top. Cover the dough loosely with oiled cling film and leave to rise for another 30 minutes. When the focaccia looks puffy, it's ready to bake.

7. Preheat the oven to 220°C/200°C fan/gas 7. When the focaccia is risen, use your fingers to press a few more indentations into the dough, drizzle with oil and sprinkle with sea salt. Bake for 20 minutes until golden brown, then remove from the tray and allow to cool on a wire rack before slicing.

Lemon and lime Battenberg

Whatever flavour you use in a Battenberg has to complement the almond it is encased in, which both lemon and lime do strikingly well. This is a unique and slightly peculiar British cake; you'd be hard pressed to find another baked good with the same psychedelic squares and level of geometric satisfaction. The unusual green-and-yellow-coloured squares are a refreshing change from the soft pink and yellow, and I love that the flavours match the colours. It's not as hard as it looks to get a perfectly formed chequerboard, but you will have to succumb to getting out the ruler and vigilantly measuring each section of cake. A great baker's perk here is gobbling up the offcuts, so keep trimming the sponge until you are happy with the dimensions.

1. Preheat the oven to 180°C/160°C fan/gas 4, grease the cake tin and line it with baking parchment, allowing the parchment to overhang at the edges. Divide the tin cavity in half by pulling up the centre of the parchment and folding a tall pleat to separate the halves. Make sure the pleat is as close to the centre as possible.

2. Cream the butter and sugar together in a bowl for 4–5 minutes, using a stand mixer or an electric hand-held whisk, until pale and fluffy. Beat in the eggs, one at a time, adding 1–2 tablespoons of the flour if the mixture curdles.

3. In a separate bowl, combine the flour and ground almonds. Gradually add the dry mixture to the wet mixture until a thick batter forms, then scoop half the mixture into a separate bowl.

4. Add the lemon juice, lemon zest and a little yellow food colouring to one half of the batter, and do the same to the other half with the lime juice, lime zest and green food colouring, mixing until fully combined.

5. Spread the lemon mixture into one half of the tin and the lime mixture into the other half, with the parchment dividing them, and bake for 20–25 minutes or until risen and golden. Allow the cakes to cool for 5 minutes in the tin, then transfer to a wire rack to cool completely.

SERVES 10

PREP TIME: 45 MINS PLUS COOLING

COOKING TIME: 20–25 MINS

225g butter, softened, plus extra for greasing
225g caster sugar
4 eggs
225g self-raising flour
50g ground almonds
Grated zest and juice of 1 unwaxed lemon
Yellow and green gel food colourings
Grated zest and juice of 1 lime
4 tbsp fine-cut lime marmalade
Icing sugar, to dust
500g block of marzipan

You will also need 20 x 20cm cake tin.

CONTINUED…

CITRUS

Lemon and lime Battenberg

6. Use a serrated knife to trim the edges off the cooled sponges. Carefully cut the sides that have coloured in the oven, as they can look off-putting if used in the Battenberg. Measure the height of the baked sponge with a ruler and slice the cake into strips the same width as the height, forming a square cross section. Mine are usually 2 x 2cm. This will create perfect squares that stack properly on top of one another.

7. Gently warm the lime marmalade in a small saucepan to loosen it and make it easier to spread, then pass it through a sieve. Stick one lemon strip of cake and one lime strip together using some of the lime marmalade, then stack the alternate colour on top of the bottom layer to create the chequerboard effect with the four strips.

8. Lightly dust the worktop with icing sugar, then roll out the marzipan into a large rectangle, trimming the edges so the rectangle is approximately 18 x 20cm. Brush the top and sides of the assembled cake with the remaining marmalade, then place top-side down on to the marzipan along the short edge. Brush the face-up side of the cake with more marmalade before tightly rolling it up in the marzipan until it is covered. Press in the final section of marzipan or trim if it looks too long.

9. Trim the ends of the cake using a serrated knife and transfer the Battenberg to a plate or cake stand. The cake will keep for up to 1 week in an airtight container.

Fruit

Understanding Fruit

Orchard, stone, berries and exotic fruits are perfect for when your body craves something refreshing and nourishing but not quite as powerful as citrus fruits – anything from creamy bananas or powerful cherries to mellow, sweet peaches or vibrant berries.

Stone fruits include some of my all-time favourites. Peaches, nectarines, plums, apricots and cherries are luscious and juicy with tender flesh and a gentle honeyed nectar. Whether shiny or fuzzy-skinned, at optimum ripeness they are delicate and sweet, perfect for poaching or eating just as they are.

Vibrant and small, berries are not to be underestimated as they can pack a punch in the flavour department. Raspberries, blackberries and cranberries are sharp and work brilliantly to lighten heavy, rich or sweet bakes. Strawberries and blueberries provide a much more fragrant flavour, which is heightened when baked. Most berries work wonderfully in jams and jellies, thanks to the high levels of pectin they contain.

Exotic fruits add a bit of a tropical twist to your baking. From punchy passionfruit to floral lychees, there is a wealth of different fruits to get stuck into and experiment with.

I try to shop locally and check what fruit is in season before planning recipes that include it. While it's possible to purchase fresh produce all year-round, blueberries in February will be more expensive and less flavoursome than their late-summer relatives.

Absorbing liquid

Dried fruits such as raisins and prunes soak up liquid and swell, which helps 'glue' together fruit cakes and other bakes. They also distribute pockets of moisture through cakes. Firm, fresh fruit that is poached absorbs the cooking liquid (spiced syrup or mulled wine, perhaps) and can take on flavourings or sweeteners added to the liquid to enhance the flavour of the fruit. *See:* (*Dried*) Persian Fruit Cake; (*Fresh*) Mulled Wine Pavlova

Gels, jams and jellies

Berries, apples and some other fruits contain a substance called pectin. When these fruits are cooked with sugar in acidic conditions, the pectin in the fruit binds with water and forms a gel, which is key to setting jams and jellies. The set depends on the pH of the fruit: some fruits contain enough acid to allow the pectin to set, but most require the addition of lemon juice to create the ideal pH.

See: Passionfruit Viennese Whirls

Flavour

Most fruits are considered to be at their best when raw, but cooking can intensify their flavours and create new and appealing textures. The flavours of different types of fruit vary wildly, from floral and sweet to clean and crisp – the multitude of fruity flavours is something I'll never tire of eating or experimenting with in my bakes. Baking or cooking fruit can also release vibrant colours: slightly dull-looking plums stewed with sugar become a deep, cherry-red with a rich flavour. *See:* Cherry and Marzipan Pie

Moisture

When fruit is puréed and added to cake batter it disperses flavour and moisture throughout the sponge, giving it a great texture. Adding moisture this way helps keep the cake soft and moist for longer. *See:* Peaches and Cream Cupcakes

Mini doughnut muffins

Fresh doughnuts are one of the things I crave most, but making yeasted doughnuts is a lengthy, involved process that I often don't have time to undertake. Doughnut muffins are my solution. Jammy and bite-sized with none of the wait, once you've made them a few times you won't even have to look up the recipe. You can use any type of jam to fill these or simply eat them plain.

MAKES 24 MINI MUFFINS
PREP TIME: 12 MINS
COOKING TIME: 7–8 MINS

100g butter
75g caster sugar, plus extra to dust
100g plain flour
½ tsp bicarbonate of soda
50g natural yoghurt
1 egg
1 tsp vanilla extract or vanilla bean paste
1 tbsp raspberry jam
1 tbsp apricot jam

You will also need a 24-hole mini muffin tray and two disposable piping bags.

1. Preheat the oven to 200°C/180°C fan/gas 6. Melt the butter in the microwave or in a pan over a medium heat and use a pastry brush to grease all the holes of the muffin tray with some of the melted butter.

2. Place the sugar, flour and bicarbonate of soda in a bowl and combine.

3. In a small jug, mix the remaining melted butter with the yoghurt, egg and vanilla. Pour the wet ingredients into the dry ingredients and gently fold them together until just incorporated.

4. Divide the mixture among the 24 holes in the muffin tray using a teaspoon, then bake for 7–8 minutes or until golden brown and risen.

5. While the muffins are baking, spoon the jams into the 2 piping bags and snip the end off each with a pair of scissors. Remove the hot doughnuts muffins from the oven and roll them in caster sugar, then make a small hole with a skewer in the bottom of each and pipe raspberry jam into the centre of half the doughnuts and apricot jam into the rest. These are best enjoyed fresh from the oven.

Quick berry crumbles

Crumble is a proper winter warmer. This is the kind of pudding that you should eat wrapped in a blanket by the fire on chilly days. You can use any type of fruit as the base of the crumble, but berries work particularly well as they soften and cook really quickly. Frozen berries can be used in place of fresh, but they will take slightly longer to soften.

1. Preheat the oven to 200°C/180°C fan/gas 6. Have 4 large ramekins or heatproof tapas dishes ready on a baking tray.

2. Combine the strawberries, mixed berries, runny honey and butter in a small saucepan over a medium heat and cook gently until the berries have softened and the juices reduce a little.

3. While the berries are softening, make the crumble topping. Place the flour, butter and sugar in the bowl of a mini food processor (I use a stick blender with a chopping attachment) and pulse until the mixture starts to clump together, then stir in the rolled oats. If you don't have a food processor or stick blender, make the crumble by hand by rubbing the butter into the flour and sugar until the mixture resembles breadcrumbs, before adding the oats.

4. When the fruit is soft and slightly reduced, divide the mixture among the 4 ramekins or dishes. Top each with the crumble mix and bake on the top shelf of the oven for 10 minutes until the crumble topping is golden brown and the fruit bubbling. Serve immediately with cream or hot vanilla custard.

SERVES 4

PREP TIME: 10 MINS

COOKING TIME: 10 MINS

100g strawberries, hulled and quartered
250g mixed berries (such as raspberries, blueberries, blackberries or blackcurrants)
2 tbsp runny honey
1 tbsp butter
Cream or hot vanilla custard, to serve

CRUMBLE TOPPING
75g plain flour
75g butter, chilled and cubed
50g soft light brown sugar
25g rolled oats

Mango and prawn filo cups

Fruit complements savoury flavours really well, especially in bite-sized canapés, where they offer a burst of freshness among rich, heavy platters. Of course, pairing sweet and savoury is not revolutionary; we've embraced the retro delight of cheese and pineapple on cocktail sticks for years.

Using filo pastry to create cups makes a great base for a range of different canapés as you can fill the cup with whatever you like. I fill mine with juicy mango, homemade sweet chilli sauce and prawns for a little mouthful with big, powerful flavours.

1. Preheat the oven to 200°C/180°C fan/gas 6 and use a pastry brush to brush a 24-hole mini muffin tin with oil.

2. Lay the 6 filo sheets on top of each other on the worktop and cut them into 16 squares. Brush each square with oil or butter and lay it in the muffin tin until each hole has 4 layers of filo. Push the filo down into the hole to form a little cup.

3. Bake the filo cups for 10–12 minutes until golden brown and crisp.

4. Place the chilli in a small saucepan, add the honey and lime juice, and stir briefly. Bring to the boil and simmer gently for a few minutes, then add the mango to the pan along with the cooked prawns and soy sauce. Cook for a further 5 minutes, making sure the prawns are heated through and well coated in the glaze. Remove from the heat, season well, then spoon into the filo cups just before serving. The cups can be served hot or cold.

MAKES 24 CANAPÉS

PREP TIME:
8–10 MINS

COOKING TIME:
10–12 MINS

½ x 270g pack filo pastry (pack cut in half)
50ml vegetable oil, plus extra for greasing, or melted butter
1 small red chilli, deseeded and finely chopped
2 tbsp runny honey
Juice of ½ lime
½ small ripe mango, peeled, stoned and cut into small chunks
200g cooked shelled prawns
1 tbsp soy sauce
Salt and freshly ground black pepper, to season

You will also need a 24-hole mini muffin tin.

Honey scones with rhubarb compote

While visiting Scotland and Northern Ireland, I found that the humble scone is quite the centre of attention. Our simple jam-and-cream offering, with the occasional raisin thrown in, doesn't quite cut it compared with the likes of treacle, cinnamon or cherry scones. This is a simple scone with a bit of a makeover: glazed with sticky honey and generously smothered in clotted cream and tart rhubarb compote.

1. Preheat the oven to 200°C/180°C fan/gas 6 and line a baking tray with baking parchment.

2. Place the rhubarb in a saucepan with the sugar and orange juice. Simmer over a medium heat for about 10 minutes, stirring occasionally, until the rhubarb pieces have completely broken down and the mixture is thick and sticky. Spoon into a small jar or ramekin and leave to cool.

3. To make the scones, place the flour in a large bowl and add the cubes of butter. Quickly rub the butter into the flour using your fingertips until the mixture resembles fine breadcrumbs. Stir in the sugar and make a well in the centre.

4. Pour the honey into the centre of the well, then gradually add the milk, stirring it into the mixture using a round-ended knife. A soft, rough dough will form. Tip the dough out on to a lightly floured worktop and knead very briefly to smooth out the dough. Over-handling the dough will make your scones tough and flat, so knead as little as possible.

5. Gently roll the dough out to a thickness of around 3cm. Cut into rounds using a 6cm pastry cutter, cutting straight down and not twisting, as twisting prevents the scones from rising properly. Very gently re-roll the remaining dough, taking care not to handle it too much, and punch out more scones – you should get 9 in total. Arrange the scones on the lined baking tray and brush the tops with a little extra honey.

6. Bake for 12–15 minutes or until risen and golden brown. Serve warm from the oven, split in half, with big dollops of clotted cream and rhubarb compote.

MAKES ABOUT 9 SCONES

PREP TIME: 30 MINS

COOKING TIME: 12–15 MINS

RHUBARB COMPOTE
200g rhubarb, trimmed and cut into small pieces
50g caster sugar
100ml orange juice

HONEY SCONES
300g self-raising flour, plus extra for dusting
75g cold butter, cubed
25g caster sugar
2 tbsp runny honey, plus extra for glazing
125ml whole milk
Clotted cream, to serve

You will also need a 6cm-round pastry cutter.

Peaches and cream cupcakes

One of the things I love most about summer is biting into ripe, juicy peaches that drip down your chin in an undignified manner. Adding fruit purée to sponges locks in moisture, which makes for a delicious soft sponge, but if you prefer you can leave the peaches in small chunks for a different texture. You can use fresh or tinned peaches to make these, but fresh will have a superior flavour.

1. Preheat the oven to 180°C/160°C fan/gas 4 and line the muffin tins with 18 muffin cases.

2. Cut the peaches into chunks and place them in a food processor or a stick blender with a processor attachment. Purée until smooth.

3. Cream the butter and sugar together in a bowl using an electric hand-held whisk or in a stand mixer fitted with the paddle attachment until really pale and fluffy – this is what will make the sponge light.

4. Add the vanilla extract to the butter and sugar mix then add the eggs, one at a time, mixing after each addition and scraping the mixture down from the sides of the bowl with a spatula. Don't worry if the mixture looks curdled at this point – it should blend together after the flour is added.

5. Combine the flour and baking powder in a small bowl. With the whisk or mixer on low speed, add half the flour mixture, followed by all the peach purée, then the remaining flour, mixing well between each addition until the mixture is smooth. It will form a very thick batter.

6. Divide the mixture evenly among the cases and bake for 20–25 minutes. The cakes should be springy to the touch and a metal skewer inserted into the centre of one of the cakes should come out clean. Remove from the oven and leave to cool completely.

7. While the cakes are cooling, make the topping. Whisk the cream and icing sugar together in a bowl until the mixture just holds its shape when you lift the whisk. If the cream is too stiff it won't spread smoothly.

8. When the cakes are at room temperature, decorate them with the cream topping using a palette knife. Put a tablespoon-sized dollop on the top of each cupcake, then smooth it down into the edges to form a cone shape. Use the rounded end of the spatula to create a swirl at the top. Decorate with a slice of fresh peach and keep chilled until ready to serve.

MAKES 18 CUPCAKES

PREP TIME: 20 MINS PLUS COOLING

COOKING TIME: 20–25 MINS

CUPCAKES
200g peeled, halved and stoned peaches (fresh or from a tin)
125g butter, softened
200g caster sugar
2 tsp vanilla extract
2 eggs
250g plain flour
2 tsp baking powder

TOPPING
300ml double cream
2 tbsp icing sugar
1 ripe peach, halved, stoned and cut into 18 slices, to decorate

You will also need 2 x 12-hole muffin tins and 18 paper muffin cases.

Sweet and sour apple crisps

Fruit crisps are one of my favourite ways to enjoy fruit on the go. Drying out thin slices of apple concentrates their flavour into intense, crispy morsels, which make a fantastic snack. I like to use a combination of different types of apple; you'd be amazed how much the flavour differs between each variety. Tart Granny Smith or Bramley apples create sour, refreshing crisps, while sweeter varieties like Pink Lady or Gala have beautiful pink edges that look stunning when they curl up in the oven. You can dust the finished crisps in sugar and cinnamon, but I prefer to eat them just as they are.

1. Preheat the oven to 120°C/100°C fan/gas ½ and line a large baking tray with baking parchment.

2. Wash and dry the apples and remove the stalk from each. Use a mandoline to carefully slice the apple horizontally into very thin slices (1–2mm thick). If you don't have a mandoline, use a sharp knife to cut slices as thinly as you can. Pop out and discard any pips. If you're not baking the apples immediately, submerge the slices in a bowl of water with a squeeze of lemon juice to stop them browning.

3. Arrange the apple slices on the baking tray, trying not to overlap the slices or they won't be so crisp. Bake for 40–50 minutes until the apples frill up at the edges and feel completely dry. They will still be fairly soft and pliable, but they will firm up and quickly become crisp as they cool.

4. Transfer the cooked apple slices to a wire rack and leave them to cool. Sprinkle over the cinnamon and sugar (if using) before serving. The crisps will keep in an airtight container for a few days, but they are best eaten while they're still fresh as they lose their crispness over time.

MAKES ABOUT 50 CRISPS

PREP TIME: 10 MINS

COOKING TIME: 40–50 MINS

1 Granny Smith apple or other cooking apple

1 Pink Lady apple or other sweet dessert apple

Juice of ½ lemon (optional)

1 tsp ground cinnamon (optional)

2 tsp caster sugar (optional)

Passionfruit Viennese whirls

If the idea of a passionfruit-flavoured, deliciously crumbly, melt-in-the-mouth biscuit doesn't make you hungry, then nothing will do! Viennese whirls are one of the bakes I can't resist. Using fine powders like icing sugar and cornflour in the biscuit dough creates a melting texture unlike that of any other biscuit, as the small particles stop the formation of gluten, which can toughen them. The biscuit will break apart in your mouth easily, making it incredibly moreish. I've used a tart passionfruit filling in my whirls because I find the usual jam and buttercream cloyingly sweet. It cuts through the buttery biscuit and sugary filling perfectly.

1. Scoop the flesh out of both passionfruits and place it in a small saucepan with the caster sugar. Simmer over a medium–high heat for 1–2 minutes or until bubbling and slightly thickened, then remove from the heat and set to one side to cool.

2. Preheat the oven to 180°C/160°C fan/gas 4 and line a baking tray with baking parchment.

3. To make the biscuits, beat the butter and icing sugar together in a bowl with a wooden spoon until smooth. Stir in the plain flour and cornflour until a thick paste forms, then beat in the vanilla and milk to loosen the mixture slightly.

4. Spoon the mixture into the piping bag and pipe 16 rounds (approximately 4cm in diameter) on to the lined baking tray.

5. Bake for 10–12 minutes until the biscuits are a pale golden colour. Remove from the oven and allow to cool for 5 minutes on the tray, then transfer to a wire rack to cool.

6. To make the buttercream, use an electric hand-held whisk to cream together the butter, icing sugar and lemon juice in a bowl until pale and light. Spread buttercream on to half the biscuits and passionfruit on to the other half, then sandwich them together.

MAKES 16 WHIRLS

PREP TIME: 25 MINS PLUS COOLING

COOKING TIME: 10–12 MINS

PASSIONFRUIT FILLING
2 passionfruits
25g caster sugar

BISCUITS
100g butter, softened
25g icing sugar
100g plain flour
25g cornflour
1 tsp vanilla bean paste or vanilla extract
1 tsp milk

BUTTERCREAM
25g unsalted butter
50g icing sugar
1 tbsp lemon juice

You will also need a piping bag fitted with a medium star nozzle.

Raspberry crepe cake

This is a therapeutic bake for lazy afternoons, as it requires a lot of repetitive pancake frying! The result is well worth it, though, and people will be impressed by the effort that's gone into it when they cut into the cake and see all the layers. Raspberry and chocolate is a classic combination but one that is well loved, and for good reason, as the sharpness of the raspberry cuts through the rich, indulgent chocolate ganache. If you've got two frying pans that are the same size, cook two crêpes at a time to speed up the bake.

1. Sift the flour and salt together into a large bowl and make a well in the centre. Whisk the milk, 75ml of water and the eggs together in a jug until well combined, then gradually pour into the well in the flour mixture, whisking all the time. Melt the butter in a small saucepan or in a small bowl in the microwave. Add 4 tablespoons of the melted butter to the crêpe batter and stir to combine.

2. Heat a small or medium frying pan over a medium–high heat. The diameter of your cake will be the same size as your frying pan, so bear this in mind when choosing the pan. Brush the pan with a little of the remaining melted butter using a pastry brush.

3. When the pan is hot, use a small ladle to spoon some batter into the pan. Swirl to coat the base of the pan, then cook the batter for about 30 seconds or until the pancake is golden on the bottom, then flip over and cook the other side for another 30 seconds. Try to make the crêpes as thin as possible. Place the cooked crêpe on to a large plate and set to one side.

4. Repeat the cooking process until you have used up all your batter, stacking the cooked crêpes on top of each other. Grease the pan every few pancakes with more of the remaning melted butter to make sure they don't stick to the pan.

5. While you are cooking the crêpes, make the raspberry cream filling. Mash three-quarters of the raspberries in a small bowl with the icing sugar to make a sauce. Beat the cream and mascarpone together until smooth, then fold in the raspberry sauce.

6. Place a crêpe on a cake stand or serving plate and spread with 2 tablespoons of the raspberry cream filling. Use a palette knife to spread the filling right to the edges. Continue to build the crêpe cake until you have used up all the crêpes and raspberry cream.

SERVES 10

PREP TIME: 30 MINS

COOKING TIME: 30–40 MINS

CRÊPES
225g plain flour
½ tsp fine salt
375ml whole milk
3 eggs
125g butter

RASPBERRY CREAM FILLING
350g raspberries
75g icing sugar
300ml double cream
250g mascarpone cheese

CHOCOLATE GANACHE
150g dark chocolate, chopped
150ml double cream
1 tbsp golden syrup

7. Now make the chocolate ganache. Place the chocolate chunks in a small heatproof bowl. Heat the cream and syrup in a small saucepan until steaming, then pour over the chocolate chunks and stir until all the chocolate has melted and the sauce is smooth.

8. Pour the chocolate ganache over the cake and use a palette knife to cover the sides. Scatter the remaining raspberries over the top of the cake, then chill until ready to serve.

Blackcurrant and peanut macarons

Peanut butter and jelly sandwiches get a high-end makeover with these macarons. It sounds like a childish combination, but the flavour matching is actually quite sophisticated. Sharp, fragrant blackcurrants marry perfectly with the salty peanut butter. It takes a fruit with boldness to be able to cut through the clagginess, and blackcurrants are one of the only fruits with a flavour powerful enough to do so.

1. Line 2 large baking trays with baking parchment and set to one side.

2. Place the ground almonds and icing sugar for the macarons in a food processor and blitz until the nuts are finely ground and well mixed into the sugar. This step is key to creating smooth, even macarons. Coarse bits of almond in the batter will make the macarons grainy. Transfer the mixture to a large bowl.

3. Mix half the egg white (60g) into the finely ground almonds and icing sugar, and stir until a stiff paste forms. Set this aside while you make the Italian meringue.

4. Place the caster sugar in a small saucepan with 3 tablespoons of water. Bring to the boil and stir until the sugar has dissolved. When the mixture is clear, stop stirring and heat until the syrup reaches 118°C on a sugar thermometer. Meanwhile, put the remaining egg white in a clean, grease-free bowl (any droplets of fat can deflate meringue). As the syrup is nearing 118°C, start whisking the egg white on a high speed in a stand mixer or in a bowl with an electric hand-held whisk until it reaches soft peaks and just holds its shape on the whisk.

5. Take the syrup off the heat as soon as it is up to temperature and, with the whisk on low, slowly start to pour the syrup down the side of the bowl into the egg whites in a steady stream. Keep whisking and try to avoid pouring the syrup on to the beaters or it will get messy. Continue to whisk on high speed until the mixture has cooled slightly and the bowl is no longer hot to touch. The meringue should be thick and glossy. Add a tiny amount of purple gel food colouring to the meringue and beat again, adding colouring until you reach your desired shade.

MAKES 35 MACARONS

PREP TIME: 45 MINS
PLUS RESTING TIME

COOKING TIME:
13–15 MINS

MACARONS
160g ground almonds
160g icing sugar
120g egg white (from about 3 large eggs)
160g caster sugar
Purple gel food colouring

PEANUT BUTTERCREAM FILLING
25g butter, softened
25g smooth peanut butter
100g icing sugar
1 tbsp milk

JAM FILLING
4 tbsp blackcurrant jam

You will also need a sugar thermometer and 2 disposable piping bags.

6. Use a spatula to scrape the meringue mixture out of the bowl and on to the almond paste in the large bowl. Fold together until the mixture runs in a thick ribbon from the spatula, disappearing back into the mix within 10 seconds. If the mixture is too thick, the piping bag will leave peaks from where you have piped and the shells will not be smooth. Spoon the mixture into one of the piping bags, snip off the tip and pipe 3cm circles on to the baking parchment (using a printed template or drawn circles as a guide) and tap the trays on the worktop a few times to disperse any air bubbles.

7. Leave the macarons to dry for at least 30 minutes at room temperature until a thin skin forms on the top; it may take a little longer if the kitchen is humid. They should no longer be sticky to the touch and will have a matt appearance. The skin allows the macarons to withstand the oven temperature for long enough to rise and let the signature 'foot' (the lacy bit at the bottom of a macaron) peek out. While you are waiting, preheat the oven to 170°C/150°C fan/gas 3.

8. Bake in the centre of the oven, one tray at a time, for 13–15 minutes. The shells should not have started to brown, but they should be firm and sound hollow when lightly tapped. Leave to cool for a few minutes before peeling off the parchment.

9. To make the peanut buttercream, beat the butter, peanut butter and icing sugar together in a bowl using an electric hand-held whisk until combined, then add the milk and beat until light and fluffy. Spoon the buttercream into the second piping bag and snip off the tip.

10. To assemble the macarons, arrange the shells in pairs. Pipe a ring of buttercream around the edge of half the macaron shells, then fill the centre of each ring with jam. Sandwich together with the other macaron shells. These macarons will keep for up to 1 week in an airtight container.

Persian fruit cake

Fruit cake seems to have earned itself a bad reputation among young people; me being one of those who can't get excited about over-rich Christmas cake and dreads being offered a creased napkin full of dry wedding cake, where the only enjoyable bit is picking the marzipan and icing off the top. However, if you are a fruit-cake hater like me, I ask you to look at this cake with fresh eyes. The Middle East produces an array of incredible dried fruits, and this cake is an ode to them; a celebration of beautiful fruits and nuts, all gently melded together by a sticky rose syrup. These are no bitter currants or raisins in this reinvented recipe – just naturally sweet fruits, aromatic peels and vibrant pistachio marzipan.

1. Grease the cake tin and line the base and sides with a double layer of baking parchment. This will stop the sides of the cake browning too much.

2. Place the dried fruits in a large saucepan. Add the lemon zest, rose water, butter, sugar and honey, and place the pan over a medium heat. Heat gently, stirring all the time, until the butter melts, then simmer for about 10 minutes. Remove from the heat and leave to cool for about 30 minutes. Preheat the oven to 160°C/140°C fan/gas 2 while you are waiting for the mixture to cool.

3. Beat the eggs into the cooled fruit mix, then stir in the flour and ground almonds until well combined. Pour the cake mixture into the lined tin and bake for 1¾–2 hours or until a skewer inserted into the centre comes out clean and the top of the cake feels dry.

4. While the cake is baking, make the rose syrup. Combine the sugar and rose water with 75ml of water in a small saucepan and simmer over a medium heat until all the sugar grains have dissolved. Cook the syrup for a further 30 seconds, then remove from the heat and allow to cool completely.

5. When the cake has been cooling for 5 minutes, pierce small holes over the surface of the fruit cake and feed it with the rose syrup, using a pastry brush to apply the syrup and letting the cake absorb as much syrup as it can. This will make the fruit cake very moist. Leave the cake to cool completely in the tin.

SERVES 16

PREP TIME: 45 MINS
PLUS COOLING

COOKING TIME:
1¾–2 HOURS

CAKE
200g prunes, cut into small pieces
150g dried figs, cut into small pieces
200g dried apricots, cut into small pieces
150g chopped dates
50g piece candied orange peel, cut into small pieces
Grated zest of 1 unwaxed lemon
1 tsp rose water
200g butter, plus extra for greasing
200g soft light brown sugar
150g runny honey
3 large eggs, beaten
200g self-raising flour
100g ground almonds

ROSE SYRUP
150g caster sugar
2 tsp rose water

PISTACHIO MARZIPAN
200g pistachio nuts
100g icing sugar, plus extra for dusting
100g caster sugar
1 large egg white
Dried rose petals and chopped pistachios, to decorate

6. To make the pistachio marzipan, blitz the pistachio nuts, icing sugar and caster sugar together in a food processor until they form a really fine powder. Add the egg white and blend again until the mixture clumps together. Wrap the marzipan in cling film until ready to use.

7. Lightly dust a worktop with icing sugar and roll out the marzipan (or roll it between 2 pieces of cling film) to make a disc the same size as the top of the cake. Press the marzipan on to the top of the cake, then sprinkle on the rose petals and chopped pistachio nuts.

You will also need a 20cm-round cake tin.

Coconut custard tart with caramelised pineapple

Coconut is one of those ingredients that has inherited the health-food label and is now rarely used in any other way, which I find sad as it can be put to good use in so many delicious bakes. It's an unusual ingredient, as it's difficult to classify as either a fruit or a nut, but I find it has a unique fresh-tasting, mellow nuttiness.

1. Start with the pastry. Place the flour and icing sugar in a large bowl and mix together until well combined. Add the butter to the dry ingredients and rub the cubes into the flour with your fingertips until the mixture resembles fine breadcrumbs. Add the egg yolk (save the white for glazing) and milk, and stir them into the flour with a round-ended knife until the mixture clumps together. Squeeze the pastry together to form a ball. Knead it briefly in the bowl, then wrap it in cling film and place in the fridge for 20 minutes so the butter in the pastry can solidify.

2. Preheat the oven to 200°C/180°C fan/gas 6 and place the tart tin on a baking tray. Lightly dust a worktop with flour and roll out the chilled pastry into a circle about 5cm wider than your tart tin (you could also do this between 2 pieces of cling film). Press the pastry into the tin, leaving the excess draped over the sides. Chill the tart for 15 minutes so it keeps its shape.

3. Prick the chilled pastry with a fork and line it with a scrunched piece of baking parchment and fill with baking beans, rice or pulses. Bake for 20 minutes, then take the tart from the oven and remove the paper and beans. Glaze the inside of the tart with the reserved egg white and bake for a further 10 minutes so the base of the pastry is crisp.

4. Remove the tart case from the oven and trim off the overhanging edges with a sharp serrated knife. Turn the temperature down to 150°C/130°C fan/gas 2.

5. To make the custard, whisk together the eggs and caster sugar in a large heatproof jug or bowl with a lip until slightly paler in colour. Heat the cream, coconut milk and vanilla together in a small saucepan until just steaming, then slowly pour into the egg mixture, whisking all the time. You should have a very smooth mixture (pass it through a sieve if there are any lumps).

6. Place the baking tray with the blind-baked tart case on it into the centre of the oven and carefully pour in the custard, filling the tart right to the top. You may not need all the filling.

SERVES 12

PREP TIME: 45 MINS PLUS CHILLING

COOKING TIME: 1 ½–1 ¾ HOURS

PASTRY
225g plain flour, plus extra for dusting
25g icing sugar
125g cold butter, cubed
1 egg, separated
1 tbsp milk

COCONUT CUSTARD
4 eggs
125g caster sugar
300ml double cream
300ml coconut milk
1 tsp vanilla bean paste

CARAMELISED PINEAPPLE
200g fresh pineapple, peeled and cored
1 tbsp caster sugar
1 tsp butter
Flaked coconut, to decorate

You will also need a 23cm loose-bottomed sandwich or tart tin.

7. Bake the tart for 1–1¼ hours or until it is set around the edges with just a slight wobble in the centre. Remove from the oven and allow to cool completely in the tin, then chill the tart until you are ready to serve.

8. Just before serving, slice the pineapple into thin pieces and sprinkle both sides of each piece with the caster sugar. Heat the butter in a small frying pan until foaming, then add the pineapple slices and cook for 1–2 minutes on each side or until nicely browned.

9. Remove the tart from the tin and decorate with the caramelised pineapple slices. Sprinkle some flaked coconut over the top before slicing and serving.

Cherry and marzipan pie

There is no hiding from the fact that making a pie from scratch requires a certain level of effort, so when I decide to invest time in making one it has to be good. Ladies and gentlemen, this pie is definitely worth it. Cherry and almond is a flavour combination that has stood the test of time, so sprucing up a classic by adding little pockets of melted marzipan is sure to be a hit with any Bakewell-tart lovers. I adore how the sticky, dark red cherry filling bubbles up between the lattice squares. The cooler your pastry is, the easier it is to create the lattice strips, so don't skip the chilling stage.

1. To make the pastry, place the flour, almonds and icing sugar in a large bowl and mix until well combined. Add the butter to the bowl of dry ingredients and rub the cubes into the flour with your fingers until the mixture resembles fine breadcrumbs. Add the egg yolk (save the white for glazing) and 1 tablespoon of cold water, and stir into the flour mix with a round-ended knife until the mixture clumps together. Turn the contents of the bowl out on to a large piece of cling film and knead briefly until all the pastry has come together into a ball. Wrap in cling film and place in the fridge for 30 minutes or until you are ready to use it.

2. Tip the cherries into a large saucepan and add the sugar, lemon juice and cornflour. Stir to combine and simmer for 4–5 minutes or until the cherries begin to soften. Tip the cherries into a sieve set over a large bowl and leave for 15 minutes to drain off and reserve any excess liquid.

3. Preheat the oven to 190°C/170°C fan/gas 5. Remove the pastry from the fridge, unwrap it and divide it into thirds.

4. Roll out two of the thirds of the pastry into a circle large enough to cover the base and sides of the pie dish. It should be about 5mm thick. Drape the pastry over a rolling pin and press it into the pie dish, then trim the edges so you are left with a 1cm overhang.

5. Sprinkle the ground almonds into the bottom of the pastry-lined dish. This will help prevent the base of the pie becoming soggy. Roll out the remaining pastry into a 20cm circle, then use a sharp knife or pizza cutter to cut 10 equal-sized strips from the dough. If the pastry starts to feel too soft to work with, chill the pastry strips and the pie dish for 15 minutes.

SERVES 8

PREP TIME: 40 MINS PLUS CHILLING

COOKING TIME: 40–45 MINS

PASTRY
200g plain flour
20g ground almonds
35g icing sugar
125g cold butter, cubed
1 egg, separated

FILLING
700g pitted black cherries (fresh or frozen)
100g caster sugar
Juice of ½ lemon
2 tbsp cornflour
1 tbsp ground almonds
150g marzipan, cut into small dice
1 tbsp caster sugar, for sprinkling
Cream or ice-cream, to serve

You will also need a 20cm-round pie dish.

6. When you are ready to assemble, transfer the strained cherries into the pie casing. Stir in 2 tablespoons of the reserved strained juice, then push the marzipan dice into the filling, making sure they are all sitting beneath the surface. Create a woven lattice across the top of the pie by first layering over 5 horizontal strips. Working quickly, interweave the remaining pastry in the opposite direction by lifting alternate strips and sliding them in.

7. Beat the reserved egg white in a small bowl and brush over the pastry as a glaze. Sprinkle over the tablespoon of caster sugar and bake for 40–45 minutes until the pastry is golden and the filling is bubbling. Allow to cool for a few minutes before serving with cream or ice-cream.

Nut

Understanding Nuts

I am a marzipan fiend; an open packet left in a drawer never lasts long in my kitchen. The sweet yet bitter almond flavour is something I crave daily – stuffed into a croissant, covering a cake, melted into fruit pies or simply rolled into balls and eaten greedily. Peanut butter or Nutella spread liberally on toast is a weakness of mine, as are roasted nuts tossed in honey and sea salt.

Nuts deserve much more time in the spotlight. They aren't just to be wheeled out at Christmas and left in a bowl to pick at or a bland healthy snack used as a substitute for delicious things like chocolate. When given proper attention, they are a food with so much to give. Each variety has a unique taste, texture and colour, which makes them brilliant for jazzing up bakes. Vibrant green pistachios, sweet creamy hazelnuts, wrinkled bitter walnuts, buttery mahogany-coloured pecans – there is always something new to try.

They are unusual ingredients that work wonderfully in sweet and savoury dishes. You'll find nuts in everything from teeth-welding brittle to satay sauce and Indian bread fillings. Nuts sprinkled over breads or rippled through cakes add a contrasting texture that is often much needed in baking.

The great thing about baking with nuts is that they all have fairly similar properties, so they can be interchanged in recipes. People can be fussy about which nuts they like, so feel free to substitute one type of nut for another in any of my recipes. You can blitz them up in the food processor to make ground nuts of all varieties – it makes a nice change from standard ground almonds.

Ground nuts

Ground nuts can create structure as well as adding flavour to a bake. Raw nuts such as almonds become flour-like when ground and can be used instead of flour in sponges, cookies and other bakes. Nut flours work best when combined with grain flours or egg, as they are naturally gluten-free so lack the bonding qualities which egg or gluten-rich flours provide. You can grind your own nuts by pulsing them in a food processor, or buy them ready-ground.
See: Blackcurrant and Peanut Macarons

Nut milks

Nut milks are made by soaking raw nuts in water (preferably overnight), then blending them to form a smooth cream. High-fat nuts such as cashews work best. Nut proteins coagulate quite easily, so the milks can be used to thicken puddings and make custards. Coconut milk is made by blitzing coconut flesh with water until smooth, then straining it through muslin. *See*: Coconut Custard Tart with Caramelised Pineapple

Nut butters and pastes

Pairing roasted nuts with a good-quality food processor offers huge possibilities – try it with different types of nut and marvel at the results. A few seconds of blitzing creates ground nuts, ready to be used in fillings or biscuits; a minute or two of blitzing with sugar and egg white creates thick marzipans; and 8–10 minutes of blitzing creates beautifully smooth nut butters, perfect for spreading on toast or using in cookies.
See: Baklava

Toasting

Toasting gets the best flavour from nuts. It is the easiest way to impart depth of flavour and true nuttiness into your bakes, as it releases the oils that lock away so much of the flavour. Simply by spreading nuts on a baking tray and baking them in the oven until golden, you transform bland, pale kernels into aromatic morsels which are perfect for baking with. *See*: Nutty Chocolate Babka

Hazelnut and chocolate spread

This is a dangerous recipe, because once you learn how simple it is to make homemade Nutella, you won't be able to stop. It's delicious on its own, spread on wholemeal toast or used in baking. You can tweak the sweetness of the spread by changing the amount of honey or percentage of the chocolate you use. I like a darker spread so I use dark chocolate. Make sure you remove the papery, bitter skins from the hazelnuts before using them or buy them blanched.

1. Preheat the oven to 200°C/180°C fan/gas 6.

2. Spread the nuts out in a single layer on a large baking tray and roast them for 6–8 minutes or until they begin to darken and smell more fragrant.

3. Tip the roasted nuts into the food processor and pulse until they are coarsely ground, then blend on full speed for 5–7 minutes, stopping every once in a while to scrape the sides down with a spatula. The paste will look dry and finely ground for a while, but be patient and the oils will eventually be teased out of the hazelnuts and they will turn into a thick, smooth paste.

4. While the hazelnuts are blending, place the dark chocolate, butter and honey in a heatproof bowl over a pan of simmering water and stir until the chocolate and butter have melted. When no lumps of butter or chocolate remain, stir in the milk. Pour the chocolate mixture into the food processor and add the salt, then continue to blend for a minute or so more, until smooth and well combined.

5. Spoon the spread into a large sterilised jar (see page 10 for sterilising method) and store in a cool, dark place for up to 1 month or use straight away as a delicious chocolate dip.

MAKES 1 LARGE JAR
PREP TIME: 10 MINS
COOKING TIME: 6–8 MINS

200g skinless or blanched hazelnuts
100g dark chocolate (I like to use 70% cocoa solids), chopped
25g butter
50g runny honey
75ml milk
Pinch of sea salt

You will also need a food processor.

Honey and sea salt roasted nuts

Making your own roasted nuts couldn't be easier, and they taste so much better than shop-bought alternatives when you make them fresh. The flavour of the nuts you use is much stronger, as the oils released when nuts are baked are not allowed time to mellow. This recipe works with any kind of nut, but peanuts and cashews are my personal favourite, as the honey and salt coating sticks to them really well. Make these in the run-up to Christmas for fantastic festive nibbles or decant them into pretty jars and give as seasonal gifts for your friends and family to enjoy.

SERVES 4 AS A SNACK
PREP TIME: 5 MINS
COOKING TIME:
10–15 MINS

25g butter
1 tbsp runny honey
½ tsp ground cinnamon
100g unsalted peanuts
100g unsalted cashews
1 tbsp granulated sugar
1 tsp flaked sea salt

1. Preheat the oven to 200°C/180°C fan/gas 6 and line a baking tray with baking parchment.

2. Melt the butter in a small saucepan with the honey and cinnamon over a medium heat, then simmer for 2–3 minutes.

3. Stir in the peanuts and cashews until they are all well coated, then tip them on to the lined baking tray and spread them out evenly. Roast in the oven for 10–15 minutes. Halfway through the cooking time, shake the tray and break up any clumps of nuts with a spoon to make sure all the nuts roast evenly and don't get too stuck together.

4. Remove from the oven and immediately sprinkle the nuts with the sugar and salt, stirring until the nuts are well coated. Allow to cool briefly on the tray so the honey can set, then serve warm in small cones or decant into a Kilner jar to give as a gift. The nuts should stay crisp for a few days and can be freshened up again by warming them in the oven for a few minutes.

Peanut butter cookies

Once I realised how little time and effort stood between me and freshly baked peanut butter cookies, I was never tempted to buy a bag of cookies from a bakery again! These cookies couldn't be simpler to make; it's just a case of mixing everything together in a bowl, then baking small balls of the dough. You can easily make these cookies gluten-free by using gluten-free flour and gluten-free baking powder in the place of plain flour. This simple dough can also be customised with chopped nuts or chocolate chips.

1. Preheat the oven to 180°C/160°C fan/gas 4 and line a baking sheet with baking parchment.

2. Beat the peanut butters and both the sugars with the vanilla extract in a bowl until fully combined. Add the beaten egg to the bowl and mix until completely incorporated.

3. Combine the flour and baking powder in a small bowl, then stir this into the peanut butter mixture. Keep mixing until a thick, stiff dough forms.

4. Use an ice-cream scoop or dessertspoon to form 12 small balls and place them on the baking sheet, leaving room for them to spread in the oven. Gently flatten each ball to help them spread.

5. Bake the cookies for 10–12 minutes, until lightly golden around the edges and still soft in the middle. Be careful not to over-bake them, as the chewy centre is what makes these cookies so delicious! Remove from the oven and allow the cookies to firm up slightly on the tray before eating. They keep well in an airtight container for up to 5 days.

MAKES 12 COOKIES

PREP TIME: 8 MINS

COOKING TIME: 10–12 MINS

125g crunchy peanut butter
100g smooth peanut butter
75g soft light brown sugar
100g caster sugar
1 tsp vanilla extract
1 egg, beaten
50g plain flour
½ tsp baking powder

Coffee bean and almond brittle

I add butter to my caramel whenever I'm making brittle. The resulting caramel is much smoother and more enjoyable to eat, as it almost melts in the mouth instead of sticking to your teeth. Salted butter creates the salted-caramel effect, and adding bitter roasted coffee beans means the brittle isn't cloyingly sweet either.

1. Preheat the oven to 200°C/180°C fan/gas 6 and line a baking tray with baking parchment.

2. Spread the chopped almonds evenly over the parchment in a single layer and bake for 4–5 minutes until they just start to toast. Sprinkle over the coffee beans and roast for a further 2 minutes. Remove the tray from the oven and set to one side.

3. Place the sugar, butter and 50ml of water in a medium saucepan. Heat gently over a low heat, stirring until all the sugar has dissolved and the butter has melted. When you can no longer see grains of sugar, stop stirring immediately and turn up the heat. Allow the mixture to bubble for 3–4 minutes until the caramel changes from pale yellow to a dark amber colour (around 150°C on a sugar thermometer, if you have one). Swirl the pan occasionally to help the caramel cook evenly, but do not stir it.

4. Remove the caramel from the heat and stir until it is smooth and no longer bubbling. Pour the hot caramel over the roasted almonds and coffee beans. Shake and tap the tray on a worktop to get a nice even layer, then leave to harden completely before snapping it into pieces. You can eat this delicious brittle as it is, or you can use it to decorate cakes or even crush down to a praline by blitzing the brittle in a food processor until finely ground (try using it in my Pecan Praline Brownies recipe on page 78).

MAKES ABOUT 15 PIECES

PREP TIME: 10 MINS PLUS COOLING

COOKING TIME: 4–5 MINS

75g skinless blanched almonds, roughly chopped
25g roasted whole coffee beans, roughly chopped
100g caster sugar
25g butter

Amaretti biscuits

There is a stall at Borough Market in London that sells legendary doughnuts, but I recently branched out and tried one of their perfectly dusted, aptly named 'Amaretti di Southwark'. Sticky like marzipan and a far cry from artificial, crunchy impostors; I knew from the moment I tried these, walking along the southern bank of the River Thames, that they would be a firm favourite and that I had to come up with my own version. Be sure to coat the biscuits liberally in icing sugar so they crack properly in the oven. They make great gifts.

1. Preheat the oven to 170°C/150°C fan/gas 3 and line a large baking sheet with baking parchment.

2. Put the egg whites in a large, clean grease-free bowl and whisk with an electric hand-held whisk or manual balloon whisk until stiff peaks form. Be warned that whisking them by hand will take considerably more time and effort!

3. Gently fold the sugar, almonds and amaretto liqueur or almond extract into the mixture, until a thick paste forms.

4. Roll the mixture into small balls using your hands, then coat each ball liberally in icing sugar – you should make about 30 biscuits – and place them on the lined baking sheet. Bake for 15–20 minutes until golden brown and cracked on top. The biscuits will keep well, stored in an airtight container, for up to 1 week.

EXPRESS

Bake miniature amaretti biscuits to use as decorations for cakes or cute snacks by rolling tiny balls of the mixture. Bake in the same way as above, reducing the cooking time to 10 minutes.

MAKES ABOUT
30 BISCUITS

PREP TIME: 15 MINS

COOKING TIME:
15–20 MINS

2 egg whites
150g caster sugar
175g ground almonds
1 tbsp amaretto liqueur
    (or a few drops of
    almond extract)
Icing sugar, to dust

Sticky maple pecan pudding

A few years ago, I had the privilege of teaching the Archbishop of Canterbury how to make sticky toffee pudding in front of a large audience of young people in a Birmingham church. While it ranks up there as one of the most surreal moments in life, the puddings we baked were gloriously sticky and raved about by those who got a little taste. This recipe is a twist on the classic, throwing in pecan nuts and maple syrup for a contrasting texture and distinctive caramelised flavour. Try pouring the maple sauce over the pudding and putting it under the grill for a few minutes before serving to achieve perfect stickiness.

1. Preheat the oven to 180°C/160°C fan/gas 4 and grease the ovenproof dish with butter.

2. Place the dates in a heatproof bowl. Pour over 50ml of boiling water, the maple syrup and bourbon (if using), and leave to soak while you make the pudding batter.

3. Beat the butter and sugar together in a large bowl with a wooden spoon or an electric hand-held whisk for a few minutes until light and fluffy. Add the eggs one at a time, beating well between each addition. Sift in the flour and bicarbonate of soda until well incorporated, then pour in the milk. Fold the soaked dates, any soaking liquid and the chopped pecans into the pudding batter.

4. Spread the pudding mixture evenly into the buttered dish and bake for 25–30 minutes until risen, golden and firm.

5. While the pudding is cooking, make the maple sauce. Put the sugar, maple syrup, butter and cream in a medium saucepan. Place over a medium heat and bring to the boil, stirring all the time, until the sugar has completely dissolved. Turn up the heat slightly and let the mixture bubble away for 2–3 minutes until it is a rich toffee colour.

6. When the pudding is cooked, sprinkle the roughly chopped pecans over the top and pour over most of the sauce, so that it covers the whole dish. If you favour a stickier top, preheat the grill to high and place the pudding under the grill for a few minutes so the sauce bubbles and the top becomes slightly crunchy. Serve immediately with the remaining maple sauce.

SERVES 8

PREP TIME: 20 MINS

COOKING TIME: 25–30 MINS PLUS GRILLING TIME (OPTIONAL)

PUDDING
150g Medjool dates, stoned and cut into small pieces
100g maple syrup
2 tbsp bourbon whiskey (optional)
100g butter, softened, plus extra for greasing
100g soft light brown sugar
2 eggs
175g self-raising flour
1 tsp bicarbonate of soda
100ml milk
100g pecans, chopped

MAPLE SAUCE
100g soft light brown sugar
75ml maple syrup
50g butter
100ml double cream
50g pecans, roughly chopped

You will also need a 1.5 litre ovenproof dish.

Frangipane puff pastry pies

These pies are crammed full of nutty frangipane and a few cranberry jewels. You can throw in any dried fruits instead of the cranberries, but the sharpness they bring is a fantastic contrast to the sweet, rich frangipane. Make your own rough puff if you've got time, but otherwise shop-bought puff pastry is a great time-saver that I don't condemn!

1. Preheat the oven to 200°C/180°C fan/gas mark 6 and line a baking tray with baking parchment.

2. Cream together the butter and sugar for the frangipane filling in a bowl using an electric hand-held whisk until pale and fluffy. Beat in the egg, followed by the vanilla and ground almonds, until you have a smooth thick paste. Stir in the dried cranberries and place the frangipane in the fridge to chill while you cut the pastry.

3. Unroll one of the sheets of puff pastry on your worktop or roll out one of the blocks into a large rectangle about 5mm thick. Use the 4cm cutter to cut out 6 rounds of pastry and arrange them on the lined baking tray, then use the 5cm cutter to cut out 6 slightly larger circles of pastry. Repeat with the second sheet or block of pastry.

4. Spoon a teaspoon of frangipane filling into the centre of each 4cm circle, leaving a 1cm border around the edges. Dab the exposed edges with water, then carefully cover with the larger pieces of pastry and press both circles of pastry together firmly to seal. If you want the pies to be really uniform in shape, cut out the filled pies again using the smaller cutter to get neat edges. Chill the pies for 20 minutes before cooking.

5. When you're ready to bake, brush the top of each pie with beaten egg yolk, pierce a hole in the centre to allow steam to escape and score the outside with a knife. Bake the pies for 15–20 minutes until golden brown and risen. Remove from the oven and serve hot or cold.

MAKES 12 PIES

PREP TIME: 20 MINS PLUS CHILLING

COOKING TIME: 15–20 MINS

PASTRY
2 x 320g sheets or blocks of all-butter puff pastry
1 egg yolk, beaten

FRANGIPANE FILLING
50g butter
50g caster sugar
1 egg
1 tsp vanilla extract
75g ground almonds
50g dried cranberries

You will also need 2 round cutters: 4cm and 5cm.

Pecan praline brownies

Toasting glossy pecans in the oven before combining them with caramel and blitzing them into a praline brings out the distinctive buttery flavour of the nuts and works brilliantly with deviously dark, gooey brownies. You can use any nut you like, but I think pecans are particularly indulgent and have a sweet richness that other nuts struggle to match.

1. Preheat the oven to 180°C/160°C fan/gas 4, grease the brownie tin and line it with baking parchment and line a baking tray with baking parchment too.

2. Put the sugars and the butter in a large saucepan, place over a medium heat and cook, stirring occasionally, until the butter has melted and the sugar has dissolved. It should lose its grainy appearance, and the butter will have completely combined with the sugar instead of being a separated layer (this takes a few minutes). Remove from the heat.

3. Add the chopped dark chocolate to the warm sugar and butter mixture and stir it in until it has completely melted. Leave to cool to room temperature.

4. While the mixture cools, make the praline. Spread the pecans on the lined baking tray and bake in the oven for 7–8 minutes until they are golden brown. Tip the sugar into a small heavy-based saucepan or frying pan and place over a medium heat. Leave the sugar to melt without stirring. After a few minutes, the edges will have started to liquefy. Swirl the pan to distribute the caramelised sugar, which will encourage the remaining dry sugar to melt. When the caramel is a dark amber colour (or 150°C on a sugar thermometer, if you have one), remove from the heat and pour the hot caramel over the roasted pecans and allow to cool completely.

5. When the brownie mixture is cool enough to touch comfortably, beat in the eggs. Add the flour and cocoa powder then stir briefly to combine. You don't want to over-beat the mixture or your brownies will become too 'cakey'. Scrape the mixture into the lined brownie tin and spread it out evenly.

6. Remove the praline from the baking tray and blitz it in a food processor or bash it with a rolling pin until it resembles a chunky powder. Sprinkle the praline in an even layer over the brownie batter.

7. Bake for 25–30 minutes or until the top is caramelised and golden. It will feel slightly under-baked, but this is what makes the brownie fudgy and chewy. Remove from the oven and leave to cool completely in the tin, either at room temperature or in the fridge, then cut into squares.

MAKES ABOUT 15 BROWNIES

PREP TIME: 25 MINS PLUS COOLING

COOKING TIME: 25–30 MINS

BROWNIES
150g soft light brown sugar
225g caster sugar
200g butter, plus extra for greasing
150g dark chocolate, chopped
3 eggs
100g plain flour
30g cocoa powder

PRALINE
50g pecans
100g caster sugar

You will also need a 20 x 35cm brownie tin.

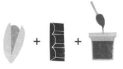

Flourless hazelnut torte

You can use any type of nut in this torte, but in my opinion you can't beat the combination of hazelnut with chocolate. If you can't get hold of ground hazelnuts, make your own by blitzing skinless, blanched hazelnuts in a food processor for a minute or two until finely ground. Tortes make fabulous desserts because they get better with time, meaning you can make them ahead, and are so rich that they serve a lot of people. The dense, buttery sponge is also gluten free, so perfect for big family gatherings to suit all dietary requirements. A simple torte looks very humble, but this one is adorned with golden caramel hazelnut spikes and a nest of glittering spun sugar set upon a cloud of whipped cream, so your efforts will not go unnoticed!

1. Preheat the oven to 180°C/160°C fan/gas 4; grease the base of the cake tin and line it with baking parchment.

2. Melt the butter and chocolate in a large heatproof bowl set over a pan of simmering water. Remove from the heat, stir in the ground hazelnuts, then allow to cool for 5 minutes.

3. Whisk the egg whites in a clean, grease-free bowl using an electric hand-held whisk until they form stiff peaks. In a separate bowl, beat the egg yolks with the sugar using the electric hand-held whisk until pale and creamy (no need to clean the whisk). Stir the egg yolk and sugar mixture into the chocolate mixture until combined.

4. Add a large spoonful of whisked egg whites to the chocolate mixture to loosen it, then use a large metal spoon or metal whisk to carefully and gently fold in the rest. Spoon the batter into the prepared cake tin, level it out and bake on the middle shelf of the oven for 35–40 minutes until the cake is risen and firm to the touch. Remove from the oven and leave the cake to cool in the tin for 15 minutes; then turn it out on to a wire rack to cool completely.

SERVES 12

PREP TIME: 1 HOUR PLUS COOLING

COOKING TIME: 35–40 MINS

125g butter, plus extra for greasing
125g dark chocolate, chopped
100g ground hazelnuts
4 eggs, separated
125g caster sugar
250ml double cream

CARAMEL-HAZELNUT SPIKES
20 skinless hazelnuts
200g caster sugar

You will also need a 20cm-round loose-bottomed cake tin and some cocktail sticks.

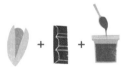

5. Make the caramel–hazelnut spikes by poking a cocktail stick into each hazelnut. Place the sugar in a medium saucepan over a low heat and stir in 2 tablespoons of water. Heat for a few minutes, stirring until the sugar has dissolved, then turn up the heat to high and stop stirring. It's important not to stir here or the caramel can crystallise. Boil until the caramel reaches a golden amber colour (around 150°C on a sugar thermometer, if you have one), then remove from the heat and allow to cool for a few minutes so it thickens to the texture of runny honey.

6. Lay a sheet of baking parchment on the floor next to a worktop, to catch the caramel drips. Dunk a hazelnut into the caramel, holding it by the stick, and make sure it is very generously coated. Wedge the cocktail stick under a heavy chopping board or heavy pan, with the nut hanging over the edge of the worktop with the parchment underneath. Allow the caramel to drip off the nut, forming a long shard, then repeat with the remaining nuts. If the caramel becomes too firm to dip, gently warm it on the hob. When the nuts are firm, trim the wispy sugar off the ends and remove the cocktail sticks. Form a nest out of the wispy sugar, breaking off any large clumps of caramel.

7. When you are ready to serve the dessert, lightly whisk the cream in a bowl so it just holds its shape, then pile it on top of the cooled torte. Just before serving, top with the spun-sugar nest and caramel–hazelnut spikes (the sugar nest will start to dissolve when it comes into contact with the cream).

Baklava

I once undertook a 21-hour bakeathon in order to raise awareness of the horrendous hours that children are forced to work in trafficking situations. I baked through the night, and my good friend and fellow *Bake Off* contestant Richard joined me for the night shift. He makes the best baklava and treated us to a tray, which we gorged on for the rest of the night to keep us going until the end of my challenge! Baklava is a beautiful, sticky Middle Eastern treat that is supposed to be enjoyed in small squares, but I guarantee that you'll be addicted from the first mouthful, and the idea of consuming just a small piece will be meaningless!

1. Preheat the oven to 180°C/160°C fan/gas 4. Place the walnuts, almonds and pistachio nuts in a food processor and blitz until the nuts form a chunky powder. Transfer to a bowl, stir in the cinnamon and set to one side.

2. Melt the butter in a small saucepan. Use a pastry brush to grease the bottom and sides of the baking tin with some of the melted butter. Unwrap the filo pastry from the packets and cover with a damp tea towel to stop it drying out or cracking.

3. Lay a sheet of filo into the bottom of your tin and brush it liberally with melted butter. Repeat the process with 5 more sheets of filo, stacking them on top of each other in the tin.

4. Sprinkle half the ground nut mixture on top of the filo, spreading it right to the edges of the tin. Top with 2 more layers of filo pastry brushed with butter, then sprinkle the remaining nut mixture into the tin. Continue to layer all the remaining filo sheets into the tin in the same way as before. Brush the top with butter and use a sharp knife to slice the baklava into diamond shapes. It is much easier to cut the baklava before it is baked and this also allows the syrup to soak right into the pastry later.

5. Bake for 30–35 minutes until the top is golden and crisp to the touch.

6. While the baklava is baking, make the syrup. Place the caster sugar in a large saucepan with the cinnamon stick, orange blossom water and 200ml of water. Bring to a gentle simmer and allow to bubble for 10 minutes or until the liquid has reduced by about a third. It should be thick and syrupy.

7. When the baklava is baked, slice through the cuts again and pour the hot syrup all over the baklava. Leave it for 2 hours at room temperature to soak in and cool completely. The baklava squares will keep well, in an airtight container, for up to 2 weeks.

MAKES ABOUT 30 PIECES

PREP TIME: 30 MINS PLUS SOAKING AND COOLING

COOKING TIME: 30–35 MINS

100g walnuts
100g almonds
50g pistachio nuts, shelled
2 tsp ground cinnamon
175g butter
12 sheets filo pastry (1 x 270g pack, sliced in two)

SYRUP
300g caster sugar
1 cinnamon stick
1 tbsp orange blossom water

You will also need a 20 x 35cm baking tin and a food processor.

NUT

Chocolate and peanut butter roulade

You can't go wrong with the combination of peanut butter and chocolate, and this roulade is a deliciously light way to enjoy it. I love the rustic look of this dessert with its irregular cracks and the way the peanut filling melds with the inner roulade. It is naturally gluten free too, so everyone will be happy.

1. Preheat the oven to 200°C/180°C fan/gas 6, then grease the Swiss roll tin and line it with baking parchment (use a shallow rectangular baking tray, if you don't have a Swiss roll tin).

2. Melt the chocolate for the roulade in a heatproof bowl set over a pan of simmering water.

3. Whisk the egg whites in a clean, grease-free bowl using an electric hand-held whisk until they form stiff peaks. Whisk the egg yolks and sugar in another large bowl (there's no need to clean the whisk) until the mixture looks pale and fluffy: it should have a thick consistency and leave a trail that holds its shape for 3 seconds when you lift the whisk out. Sift in the cocoa powder and gently fold in the melted chocolate using a spatula.

4. Spoon a small quantity of the whisked egg whites into the chocolate mixture and stir to combine. This loosens the mixture and makes it easier to incorporate the rest of the egg white. Gently fold through the rest of the white until well combined and there are no large white lumps in the mixture.

5. Pour the roulade batter into the prepared tin and spread it right to the edges. Bake the roulade for 15–20 minutes until the top feels slightly crisp and firm. Remove from the oven and leave the roulade to cool completely in the tin.

6. To make the filling, beat the cream cheese, peanut butter and icing sugar together in a large bowl with a wooden spoon or spatula. Pour in the cream and continue to beat until the mixture is smooth and thick enough to spread.

7. Lay out a sheet of baking parchment on a worktop and dust it with icing sugar and cocoa powder. Turn the roulade out on to the dusted sheet and peel off the sheet of baking parchment. Spread the peanut butter–cream filling all over the top in one even layer, using a palette knife or spatula. Sprinkle the chopped peanuts along the short edge, from which you will start rolling, to create a nutty centre. Roll up the roulade – expect it to crack a little – and dust with more cocoa and icing sugar, if you like, before serving.

SERVES 8

PREP TIME: 40 MINS
PLUS COOLING

COOKING TIME:
15–20 MINS

ROULADE
Butter, for greasing
150g dark chocolate, chopped
5 eggs, separated
150g caster sugar
2 tbsp cocoa powder, plus extra for dusting
Icing sugar, to dust

FILLING
150g full-fat cream cheese
100g smooth peanut butter
3 tbsp icing sugar
150ml double cream
50g salted roasted peanuts, finely chopped

You will also need a Swiss roll tin or shallow rectangular baking tray.

Peshwari naan breads

Is there a better Indian bread than the Peshwari naan? Not that I have tasted. Naan bread is really simple to make and cooks incredibly quickly, so I often make my own to serve with a homemade curry.

1. Place the flour in a large bowl, or the bowl of a stand mixer fitted with the dough-hook attachment, and add the yeast to one side of the bowl and the salt and sugar to the other. If you put the salt directly onto the yeast it may kill it, which will stop your dough from rising.

2. Combine the water, melted butter or ghee and the yoghurt in a bowl. Gradually pour this mixture into the bowl with the flour. Mix together, using a spoon, your hands or the dough-hook attachment, until a soft and sticky dough forms. If the dough looks dry, add a little more water.

3. Dust your worktop lightly with flour, tip the dough out on to it and knead for 10 minutes (or knead it using the dough hook on the stand mixer), until the dough is smooth and elastic. Drizzle a little oil into the bowl you used to mix the dough together, then place the dough back into the bowl, cover with a tea towel or cling film, and leave to rise at room temperature for 1–3 hours or until doubled in size.

4. While the dough is rising, make the Peshwari filling. Finely chop the sultanas so they almost resemble a paste, then add them to a small bowl with the ground almonds, desiccated coconut, caster sugar and melted butter or ghee. Stir together then set to one side.

5. Preheat your grill to high and place a large baking tray under the grill to heat up. Tip the risen dough out of the bowl and fold it in on itself a few times to remove any irregular air pockets, then divide into 8 balls. Take one of the balls of dough and roll it out into a large circle. Cover the remaining dough with a damp tea towel to stop it drying out. Sprinkle a few teaspoonfuls of the filling into the centre of the dough circle, then fold the edges to completely seal the filling inside the ball of dough. Gently roll the filled dough out into an oval shape. You want the dough to be thin, but not so thin that the filling breaks out.

6. Lay the dough on the hot baking tray and grill for 2 minutes, turning it once halfway through the time, until the bread is pale with a few dark brown spots. Don't over-cook this bread until it is dark brown or it will be crunchy rather than soft.

7. Glaze the naan bread with melted butter or ghee as soon as it comes out from under the grill, then repeat with the remaining dough. Wrap the naan breads in tin foil to keep warm while you cook the rest.

MAKES 8 NAAN BREADS

PREP TIME: 45 MINS PLUS PROVING TIME

COOKING TIME: 20 MINS

400g strong plain flour, plus extra for dusting
1 x 7g sachet fast-action dried yeast
1 tsp fine salt
1 tsp caster sugar
150ml water
2 tbsp melted butter or ghee
150g natural yoghurt
Oil, for greasing

FILLING
25g sultanas
25g ground almonds
25g desiccated coconut
1 tbsp caster sugar
1 tbsp melted butter or ghee, plus extra to glaze

NUT

85

Nutty chocolate babka

Babka is an Eastern European bread that people in the UK are raving about, and I'm not surprised. It's sticky and rich with a nutty chocolate flavour and has such an interesting appearance with the bread twisted and the filling out on display. Eating a slice while it is still slightly warm is an experience to be savoured. Be warned – once you've delved into the first slice you won't be able to stop eating until the entire loaf is demolished. This isn't a quick bake and shouldn't be rushed, but you'll consider it as time well spent when you cut into the finished loaf. To make the project more manageable I recommend chilling the dough overnight. This improves the overall flavour of the babka and allows the butter to firm up, making the dough much easier to roll out.

1. Place the flour in a large bowl, or the bowl of a stand mixer fitted with the dough-hook attachment, and add the yeast to one side of the bowl and the salt and sugar to the other. If you put the salt directly on the yeast it may kill it, which will stop your dough from rising.

2. Combine the milk and egg in a small jug, then gradually pour the mixture into the bowl with the flour, mixing all the time using your hands or the dough-hook attachment, until a stiff dough forms. Melt the butter, pour it into the dough and mix thoroughly until it is all worked in and the dough is smooth and stiff.

3. Dust the worktop with flour, tip out the dough and knead it for 5 minutes (or use the dough hook on the stand mixer) until it comes together to form a ball. Grease the bowl you used to mix the dough together with oil, then place the dough back into the bowl, cover with cling film or a tea towel and leave to rise for at least 3 hours at room temperature or overnight in the fridge. The dough will rise slowly but won't fully double. If you chill the dough overnight, make sure to bring it back to room temperature before using.

4. While the dough is rising, make the filling. Place the butter and brown sugar in a small saucepan over a medium heat, stirring until the butter has melted, the sugar has dissolved and the mixture is no longer grainy. Remove from the heat and stir in the chocolate until completely melted, then mix in the cocoa powder.

MAKES 1 LOAF

PREP TIME: 1 HOUR
PLUS PROVING TIME

COOKING TIME:
30–35 MINS

DOUGH
300g strong white bread flour, plus extra for dusting
1 x 7g sachet fast-action dried yeast
1 tsp fine salt
50g caster sugar
100ml milk
1 egg
75g butter, plus extra for greasing
Oil, for greasing

FILLING
100g butter
150g soft light brown sugar
75g dark chocolate, chopped
2 tbsp cocoa powder
100g toasted mixed nuts (I use almonds, hazelnuts and pecans), roughly chopped

SYRUP
75g soft light brown sugar

You will also need a 1 litre loaf tin.

CONTINUED...

NUT

Nutty chocolate babka

5. Tip the risen dough out of the bowl on to a lightly floured worktop and roll it out into a large rectangle about 50cm long and as wide as you can make it. Spread the chocolate mixture over the surface of the dough, right to the edges, then sprinkle the nuts over in an even layer. Roll the dough up tightly into a log shape, beginning the spiral from the 50cm end.

6. Use a sharp knife to cut the dough in half lengthways. Twist the 2 pieces of dough together in a rope-like formation, with the filling pointing outwards. Pinch the edges together at both ends to seal the loaf.

7. Grease the loaf tin with butter and line it with a strip of baking parchment that overhangs at the edges (this will make it easier to remove the loaf), then place the babka into the tin. You might need to squash the dough slightly to make it the right size for the tin – it should fit tightly. Cover the babka with a damp tea towel or plastic bag and leave to rise at room temperature for 1–2 hours, until the dough looks puffy and slightly risen.

8. While the babka is proving, make the syrup. Combine the sugar and 75ml of water in a small saucepan, and heat until the sugar has dissolved and you can no longer see any grains. Remove from the heat and allow to cool completely.

9. When you are almost ready to bake the babka, preheat the oven to 200°C/180°C fan/gas 6. Bake the babka for 15 minutes, then reduce the oven temperature to 180°C/160°C fan/gas 4 and bake for a further 15–20 minutes. If the loaf is baking unevenly, rotate it once halfway through the baking time. If the filling on the top is starting to burn, cover the loaf with a sheet of tin foil.

10. When the loaf is baked, remove it from the oven and brush it with the syrup. It may look like a lot of liquid to pour over the loaf, but it will keep the babka deliciously moist. Allow to cool completely in the tin before slicing and enjoying. The babka will keep for up to 3 days.

Spice

Understanding *Spices*

I was unsure whether to include spice as a craving, but when I thought about warm cinnamon rolls on a winter's night, wedges of sticky ginger cake with cold milk and hot fries coated in spicy salt, I knew it had earned its place.

There are so many different spices with which to bake; it's a great opportunity for experimentation and a quest to discover the ones that you love. Enrich your batters and doughs with earthy cumin, fruity star anise or woody cinnamon, and the range of flavours will astound you. Spices truly transform the simplest of bakes – you just need a small pinch to impart a bold flavour and create a delicious aroma.

It is said that we crave spice because we seek the memorable experience of that flavour. When the air is heavy with cloves and pans of mulled wine fill the kitchen with steam, these are the recognisable spices that conjure up Christmas. When cinnamon-scented dough studded with citrus peel and sultanas is shaped into buns, branded with white crosses and baked until golden brown, the unmistakable smell of Easter weaves its way through the whole house. Spices have an extraordinary way of embodying events, and you only have to unscrew the lid of a spice jar and inhale to be transported back.

Bold spicy foods have the ability to anchor themselves in our memories in a way that bland foods just can't. They demand that you pay attention to them and then keep reminding you of how good they were! To add to that, when you eat spicy foods, endorphins are released, which create a mildly euphoric feeling that lifts your mood and relieves stress. What's not to like?

Infusing

Incorporating spices such as cardamom, cloves or cinnamon into melting butter and sugar syrups is a simple but effective way of adding flavour. Use whole spices here for the strongest flavour, but remove them before eating. Infused butters and syrups are often brushed over finished bakes, allowing the flavours from the spices to of soak into every crumb. *See*: Cardamom Knots

Flavour

Spices, as well as possessing powerful flavours, can enhance existing flavours in other foods. Instead of using salt as a seasoning, try experimenting with different spices to banish blandness from food. Toasting some spices, such as cumin, fennel or coriander seeds, before you use them coaxes out their deep, earthy flavours. Simply toss in a dry, hot frying pan until aromatic, then remove from the heat and grind to a powder or use as you would any other spices. *See*: Cumin and Sesame Crackers

Aroma

The first thing that hits you when you're sitting in front of a heavily-spiced bake is the heady aroma. Every spice has a unique smell, ranging from pungent and warm ginger and paprika to earthy and nutty cumin. It's thought that 80% of perceived flavour is determined by smell, so baking with spice and having the aroma fill the room while it's in the oven is guaranteed to make you hungry. *See*: Gingerbread Blondies

Colour

Paprika, turmeric and chilli are bold in flavour and their colours reflect that. Some spices, such as saffron, are used largely because they impart a striking colour to breads and cakes as well as infusing flavour throughout. Brightly coloured spices make foods look vibrant and appealing. It is really easy to tell how evenly a colourful spice is dispersed through a bake, so incorporate it evenly. *See*: Piri-piri Popcorn

Plain popcorn

Making popcorn from scratch has become a bit of a lost art, and there's a false belief that it must be really tricky because so many of us buy microwave popcorn or ready-popped corn. Homemade popcorn is unbelievably easy to make and is the perfect base for so many different flavours. Try it freshly popped and buttered, sprinkled with cinnamon sugar or smoked sea salt for a really simple and satisfying snack, or try two of my favourite varieties, opposite and below.

SERVES 2 AS A SNACK
PREP TIME: 5 MINS
**COOKING TIME:
7–8 MINS**

1 tbsp olive oil
50g popping corn

1. Put a large heavy-based saucepan (preferably one with a glass lid) over a medium heat and add the olive oil.

2. Allow the oil to heat up for about 1 minute, then add the popping corn. Put the lid on and swirl the pan to coat the kernels in oil. Heat the popcorn, shaking occasionally, until it starts to pop. When you hear the first few pops, hold the lid on tightly and shake until the majority of the kernels have popped.

3. Once the popping has slowed to 2–3 seconds between pops, remove from the heat and tip into a large bowl. Make sure you remove any unpopped kernels before seasoning.

Oriental satay popcorn

This is an unusual popcorn recipe, but one that I make again and again because the flavour is sublime. Satay is an old favourite at Chinese and Thai restaurants, and works brilliantly as a spicy coating for popcorn.

25g butter
25g smooth peanut
 butter
1 tbsp runny honey
1 tbsp soy sauce
Juice of ½ lime
½ tsp 5-spice powder
1 x batch of plain popcorn
 (see above)

1. Melt the butter, peanut butter and honey in a small saucepan until bubbling and smooth. Remove from the heat and stir in the soy sauce, lime juice and 5-spice powder.

2. Tip the popcorn into a large container with a lid (the saucepan you popped the corn in will work) and drizzle over the satay sauce. Put the lid on and shake the pan to coat the popcorn with the sauce, then tip out on to a baking tray and allow to harden.

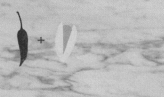

Piri-piri popcorn

Dripping with butter and tossed in spicy garlic salt, this variety of popcorn makes a great alternative to a packet of crisps and can be made in minutes.

25g butter
1 tsp sea salt
½ tsp smoked paprika
¼ tsp cayenne pepper
¼ tsp garlic granules
1 x batch of plain popcorn
   (see opposite)

1. Melt the butter in a small saucepan or in the microwave. Mix together the salt and spices in a small bowl.

2. Tip the popcorn into a large container with a lid (the saucepan you popped the corn in will work) and drizzle over the melted butter. Put the lid on and shake the pan to coat the popcorn, then sprinkle over the spice mixture. Shake again until each piece of popcorn is completely coated.

Snickerdoodle cookies

As funny as they sound, these biscuits are a fantastic quick recipe to have up your sleeve. Roll the balls of dough liberally in the cinnamon sugar so that it forms a dark shell for the pale cookies to break through. Blitz them in a food processor to speed up the prep time and try to make them no larger than a teaspoon in size so they bake quickly.

1. Preheat the oven to 200°C/180°C fan/gas 6, then line 2 large baking sheets with baking parchment.

2. Put all the cookie ingredients in a small food processor and blitz until a rough dough forms. Scrape down the sides of the bowl a couple of times during blending to make sure all the ingredients are incorporated. Give the dough a final mix with a wooden spoon to smooth out any lumps. If you don't have a food processor you can still make these cookies by beating together the butter, sugar and syrup in a bowl until smooth, then incorporating the dry ingredients.

3. Mix together the cinnamon and caster sugar for the coating in a small ramekin. Use a teaspoon and your hands to roll about 24 small balls of dough, then roll the balls in the cinnamon sugar, making sure they are really well coated. Arrange on the baking sheets, leaving room for them to spread out. You should be able to get 12 cookies on each sheet.

4. Bake the cookies for 6–8 minutes or until they have spread out and the tops look slightly cracked. Remove from the oven – they will look puffy and undercooked in the middle but will firm up on the sheets as they cool.

EXPRESS

Once you've made the dough up to step 3, it can be chilled until you're ready to bake. It will keep in the fridge for up to 4 days. You can also roll the dough into balls and freeze them for up to 1 month. Simply roll in cinnamon sugar and bake from frozen at 180°C/160°C fan/gas 4 for 12–14 minutes whenever you need a cinnamon hit.

MAKES 24 SMALL COOKIES

PREP TIME: 8–10 MINS PLUS COOLING

COOKING TIME: 6–8 MINS

COOKIES
75g butter, softened
100g caster sugar
2 tbsp golden syrup
125g plain flour
½ tsp bicarbonate of soda
½ tsp baking powder

COATING
1 tbsp ground cinnamon
1 tbsp caster sugar

Fire fries with raita dip

Spicy chips like these fries are always on sale at food festivals around the country, and I can never resist a cone-full, regardless of how stuffed I am from the countless little snacks I've eaten throughout the day. I call them fire fries because the spicy coating can make your lips tingle with the heat, while the raita dip helps to put out the fire!

1. Preheat the oven to 240°C/220°C fan/gas 8.

2. Place the fries in a large plastic bag and add the chilli oil, then shake the bag to coat the fries.

3. Mix together the spices, salt and lemon zest in a small bowl, then add them to the bag. Shake again until the fries are completely coated in the spice mix.

4. Arrange the fries on a large baking tray, leaving a small space in between each one so they can become properly crisp. If any fries are overlapping they will take longer to cook.

5. Bake on the top shelf of the oven for 10–12 minutes or until a pale golden brown colour.

6. To make the raita dip, mix together the yoghurt, cucumber and spices, and season with salt and pepper to taste. Stir in half the chopped coriander.

7. When the fries are cooked, remove them from the oven, sprinkle with the remaining fresh coriander and the fresh chilli (if using), and serve immediately with the dip and a squeeze of lemon.

EXPRESS

If you're desperate for fries and have a deep-fat fryer on hand, you can make these even faster by frying the chips as directed on the packet before coating with the spices after cooking instead of before!

SERVES 2 AS A SNACK
PREP TIME: 5 MINS
COOKING TIME: 10–12 MINS

300g frozen French fries
2 tbsp chilli oil
2 tsp garam masala
½ tsp cayenne pepper
¼ tsp garlic salt
1 tsp salt
Grated zest of ½ unwaxed lemon
½ red chilli, deseeded and finely chopped (optional)
Lemon wedge, to serve

RAITA
4 tbsp natural yoghurt
50g cucumber, deseeded and finely chopped
¼ tsp ground coriander
¼ tsp ground cumin
Small handful fresh coriander, finely chopped
Salt and pepper, to season

Gingerbread blondies

Brownies love to take all the glory as our favourite chocolate traybake, but I think blondies are a strong, often overlooked contender. They have a deep butterscotch flavour from the brown sugar, which I've used as a base for a spicy gingerbread to give these blondies a bit of a kick. Blondies keep really well and actually improve with age, so they are a great treat to bake in advance and enjoy over a whole week.

1. Preheat the oven to 180°C/160°C fan/gas 4; grease the brownie tin then line it with baking parchment.

2. Place the butter and sugar in a large saucepan and heat through until the mixture has completely melted. Remove from the heat and allow to cool to room temperature – if you don't allow the mixture to cool, the eggs will scramble when you add them.

3. Beat the eggs into the cooled mixture using a wooden spoon. Sift the flour, baking powder and spices into the pan and mix until well combined. Stir through the white chocolate chunks, then scrape the mixture into the prepared tin and spread it out evenly.

4. Bake for 20–25 minutes until firm around the edges but still slightly soft in the centre, then remove from the oven and allow to cool completely in the tin before cutting into squares. Blondies take a few hours to set to their optimum texture and actually taste their best when they are a few days old. I can never resist one warm, gooey slice when they come out of the oven, but leave the rest to set and you won't regret it. These blondies will keep well, stored in an airtight container, for up to 1 week.

MAKES 12 SQUARES

PREP TIME: 15 MINS PLUS COOLING

COOKING TIME: 20–25 MINS

150g butter, plus extra for greasing
300g soft dark brown sugar
2 eggs
200g plain flour
½ tsp baking powder
2 tsp ground ginger
1 tsp ground cinnamon
¼ tsp ground cloves
100g white chocolate, cut into small chunks

You will also need a 25 x 30cm brownie tin.

Spiced milk and honey cake

A land flowing with milk and honey is said to be a wonderful place, so naturally a delicately spiced cake full of milk and honey is a comforting treat. You couldn't ask for much more than a big slab of moist sticky cake made with these two almost nostalgic ingredients.

SERVES 10

PREP TIME: 20 MINS

COOKING TIME: 30–35 MINS

150g butter, plus extra
    for greasing
100g soft light brown
    sugar
100g runny honey
175g plain flour
1 tsp baking powder
1 tsp bicarbonate of soda
1 tsp ground cinnamon
½ tsp ground nutmeg
100ml milk
2 large eggs

HONEY GLAZE
100g icing sugar
1 tbsp milk
1 tbsp runny honey
Ground cinnamon, to dust

You will also need a
20cm-round cake tin

1. Preheat the oven to 180°C/160°C fan/gas 4, then grease the cake tin and line it with baking parchment.

2. Melt the butter, sugar and honey together in a large saucepan over a low heat until the mixture no longer appears grainy and the butter has completely melted. Remove from the heat and allow to cool slightly.

3. Combine the flour, baking powder, bicarbonate of soda and spices in a small bowl. Stir the milk into the butter mixture, then beat in both of the eggs. Sift in the dry ingredients and whisk until a smooth batter forms, then pour the mixture into the prepared tin.

4. Bake the cake for 30–35 minutes or until the top of the cake is firm and a skewer inserted into the centre comes out with a few sticky crumbs attached but no raw batter. Remove the cake from the oven and leave to cool for 5 minutes in the tin.

5. To make the glaze, mix the icing sugar, milk and honey together to make a thick icing. Pour it over the hot cake, then sprinkle the top of the cake with a light dusting of cinnamon. Leave it to cool in the tin before serving. This cake is delicious served warm or will keep for a few days in an airtight container.

Speculoos cookies

If you haven't heard of speculoos cookies, you have more than likely already tried them without knowing it, in the form of Lotus Biscoff biscuits, which are often placed on the saucer with a cup of coffee in a café, ready for you to dunk with. I like them either wafer thin or blitzed up into a delicious spread.

1. Place the flour, sugar and spices in a food processor and blitz until there are no large lumps of sugar remaining. Add the butter and pulse until the mixture resembles fine breadcrumbs. You can also do this step without a food processor by combining all the ingredients in a large bowl and rubbing the butter into the flour with your fingertips, as if you were making pastry. Add the egg and pulse in the processor or stir in by hand until a thick dough forms.

2. Shape the dough into a ball and wrap it in cling film, then place in the freezer for 15 minutes to chill. The colder your dough is, the better it will hold its shape when baking.

3. While the dough is chilling, preheat the oven to 200°C/180°C fan/gas 6 and cut a sheet of baking parchment the same size as your baking sheet and lay it on a worktop.

4. Remove the dough from the freezer, unwrap it, cut it in half and place one half in the centre of the baking parchment. Cover with a sheet of cling film and roll out the dough to a thickness of about 3mm. As the cookies are so thin, this is the best way to roll as the dough is very delicate. Peel off the cling film and cut out shapes from the dough using a small round or flower cutter, but don't lift the biscuits off the paper. Leave 1cm between each biscuit as you cut. Re-cover with the cling film and chill the sheet for 10 minutes so that it's easier to remove the excess dough. When the dough has firmed up, pull away the surrounding dough, leaving just the biscuit shapes on the parchment, then place on the baking sheet. Roll out any remaining dough and the other half of dough in the same way on another sheet of baking parchment.

5. Bake the cookies for 8–10 minutes until golden brown around the edges but soft in the middle. Remove from the oven and leave to cool. The cookies will firm up as they cool, becoming crisp. They will keep, stored in an airtight container, for up to 1 week.

MAKES ABOUT 50 COOKIES

PREP TIME: 25 MINS PLUS CHILLING TIME

COOKING TIME: 8–10 MINS

250g plain flour
175g soft dark brown sugar
1 tsp ground cinnamon
½ tsp ground nutmeg
½ tsp ground cloves
1 tsp ground ginger
150g cold butter, cubed
1 egg, beaten

You will also need a small round flower cutter.

Speculoos cookie spread

I know, biscuit spread does sound a little peculiar, but it's completely irresistible slathered on toast or used as a dip.

1. Sterilise a large jar (see instructions on page 10 for sterilising method). Melt the butter in a small pan or in the microwave.

2. Blitz 200g baked speculoos cookies in a food processor until they form fine crumbs. Add the soft dark brown sugar, honey, melted butter and 2 tablespoons of water and blitz again for a few minutes until the mix becomes creamy.

3. Spoon into the sterilised jar and store in the fridge for up to 2 weeks.

1 tbsp butter
200g speculoos cookies
1 tbsp soft dark brown
   sugar
1 tbsp runny honey

Chilli chocolate churros

If I'm honest, to me school trips to Spain were just an excuse to hunt for the best churros! In fact, I even found out that I was one of the 12 bakers chosen for *The Great British Bake Off* midway through a churro in a café in Segovia. Churros are essentially a fried choux pastry dough with deep ridges that is the perfect carrier for sugar and thick chocolate sauce. Adding chilli creates a flavour sensation.

1. Heat the butter, sugar and salt with 200ml of boiling water in a large saucepan until bubbling and the butter has melted. Remove from the heat and vigorously beat in the flour until the mixture forms a smooth ball. Set aside to cool for 5–10 minutes.

2. Add the egg to the cooled dough and beat it in by hand with a wooden spoon, or with an electric hand-held whisk, until the mixture is smooth – the batter will be very thick.

3. Line a baking sheet with baking parchment. Fill the piping bag with the batter and pipe 8–10 teardrop shapes on the parchment. The batter will be quite stiff, but persist with piping it.

4. Pour the oil into a large saucepan over a medium heat until it reaches 180°C (or sizzles when you drop in some batter). Carefully drop the churros into the hot oil, 2–3 at a time. They might sink, but they will rise as they cook. Fry for 3–4 minutes, turning occasionally with tongs, until an even, golden brown colour on both sides.

5. Remove the churros from the oil and pat them dry with kitchen paper, then continue frying the remaining churros. Mix the sugar, cinnamon and chilli powder together in a small bowl, then sprinkle the mixture over the hot churros until they are nicely coated.

6. To make the chocolate sauce, place the chocolate, cream and syrup in a small saucepan over a low heat, stirring, until melted and smooth. Remove from the heat and stir in the butter, then pour into a small heatproof bowl. Dip the churros into the warm sauce.

EXPRESS

Once you've made your churros batter and spooned it into a piping bag, you can chill the bag for up to 3 days. When you want a fresh churro, simply heat up your oil as directed above and pipe the batter straight into the oil, snipping it with scissors when the churros are your desired length. Fry until golden brown (smaller churros will cook much more quickly).

MAKES 8–10 CHURROS

PREP TIME: 20–25 MINS

COOKING TIME: 25–30 MINS

25g butter
1 tbsp caster sugar
¼ tsp salt
125g plain flour
1 egg, beaten
1 litre vegetable oil, for frying

COATING
50g caster sugar
½ tsp ground cinnamon
½ tsp chilli powder

CHOCOLATE SAUCE
100g dark chocolate, chopped
150ml double cream
1 tbsp golden syrup
25g butter

You will also need a piping bag fitted with a large star nozzle.

Pumpkin spice cupcakes

I adore carrot cake, but I'm often too lazy to be bothered to grate my own carrots. Pumpkin spice cupcakes are my secret weapon; they feature all my favourite flavours from carrot cake but none of the grating effort as the purée comes ready-made and makes the cakes incredibly moist. Pumpkin has a similar sweet flavour to carrot, so it makes a great substitute. Top with a drizzle of caramel sauce and a dusting of cinnamon for a decadent treat.

1. Preheat the oven to 180°C/160°C fan/gas 4 and line the muffin tins with the paper cases.

2. Beat together the pumpkin purée, eggs, vegetable oil, milk and both sugars in a large mixing bowl until they are well combined.

3. In another bowl, combine the flour, bicarbonate of soda, salt and spices. Fold the dry ingredients into the wet ingredients and mix until smooth, making sure that there are no large lumps of flour.

4. Divide the cake batter among between the cupcake cases (I find using an ice-cream scoop makes this easy) and bake for 25–30 minutes or until the cakes are risen and golden and a skewer inserted into the centre comes out clean. Remove from the oven and allow the cakes to cool in the tin for a few minutes, then remove from the tin and leave to cool completely on a wire rack.

5. To make the cream cheese icing, beat the cream cheese with the vanilla extract and icing sugar in a bowl either with an electric hand-held whisk or by hand using a standard whisk, until smooth. Pour in the double cream and whisk again until the mixture is thick enough to pipe. Spoon the icing into the piping bag fitted with the nozzle then pipe a zigzag of icing over the top of each cooled cupcake. Dust the cupcakes with a little cinnamon and drizzle with caramel sauce to finish. Store these cakes in the fridge until ready to eat. They will keep, chilled, for up to 3 days.

MAKES 18 CUPCAKES

PREP TIME: 15 MINS PLUS COOLING

COOKING TIME: 25–30 MINS

CUPCAKES
200g pumpkin purée (fresh or tinned)
2 eggs
100ml vegetable oil
75ml milk
125g caster sugar
125g soft light brown sugar
250g plain flour
1 tsp bicarbonate of soda
½ tsp fine salt
1 tsp ground cinnamon, plus extra to dust
½ tsp ground ginger
¼ tsp ground nutmeg
Caramel sauce, to drizzle

CREAM CHEESE ICING
200g full-fat cream cheese
1 tsp vanilla extract
75g icing sugar
150ml double cream

You will also need 2 x 12-hole muffin tins, 18 paper cases and a piping bag fitted with a large closed-star nozzle.

Cumin and sesame crackers with whipped goat's cheese

Earthy cumin and coriander seeds make these crackers more memorable than your usual cheese-and-cracker fare. Eat them with any cheese that takes your fancy – I like creamy goat's cheese spread to mellow out the strong spices.

MAKES ABOUT 30 CRACKERS

PREP TIME: 15 MINS

COOKING TIME: 9–12 MINS

1. Preheat the oven to 210°C/190°C fan/gas 6 and line a baking sheet with baking parchment.

2. Grind the cumin, coriander and sesame seeds with the peppercorns and salt in a pestle and mortar until they form a coarse powder, then stir in the sugar.

3. Melt the butter over a low heat in a small saucepan, then remove from the heat and leave to cool briefly. Place the flour in a large bowl and stir through the ground spice mixture.

4. Make a well in the centre of the flour and slowly pour in the butter and 4–5 tablespoons of cold water. Mix until a rough dough forms, kneading it briefly in the bowl to smooth out the mixture.

5. Tip the dough out of the bowl on to a lightly floured worktop. Roll out the dough to a thickness of 0.5cm, prick it evenly all over with a fork, then cut out 5cm circles (you'll get about 30 in total). Arrange the dough circles on the lined baking sheet.

6. Bake the crackers for 9–12 minutes until golden brown and crisp, then remove from the oven and transfer them to a wire rack to cool completely.

7. To make the whipped goat's cheese spread, crumble the cheese into a small bowl and add the cream cheese and chopped coriander, and season with salt and pepper to taste. Whisk using a balloon whisk until smooth, then serve alongside the crackers.

CRACKERS

1 tsp cumin seeds
1 tsp coriander seeds
1 tbsp sesame seeds
1 tsp black peppercorns
1 tsp flaked sea salt
1 tsp sugar
50g butter
150g plain flour, plus extra for dusting

GOAT'S CHEESE SPREAD

150g soft goat's cheese
75g full-fat cream cheese
Handful fresh coriander, chopped
Sea salt and black pepper

You will also need a 5cm-round cutter.

Sugar and spice doughnuts

These are fairground doughnuts – the kind you queue for late at night at festivals and eat hot straight out of the paper bag. They sell them in bags of five, and you promise yourself you'll share them with friends but you scoff the whole bag yourself instead. These doughnuts are made without yeast, so they are a lot faster to knock up and have a melt-in-the-mouth texture.

1. Cream together the butter and sugar in a large bowl using a wooden spoon or an electric hand-held whisk until light and fluffy, then beat in the egg.

2. Combine the flour, baking powder, salt and spices in a small bowl. Add half the dry ingredients to the creamed butter and sugar, followed by half of the milk, beating well after each addition. Repeat with the remaining dry ingredients and milk until a rough dough forms and all the ingredients are well incorporated.

3. Tip the dough out of the bowl on to a lightly floured worktop and knead it briefly until smooth. If the dough is too sticky to roll out, add a little more flour and knead to combine. Roll out the dough to a thickness of 1.5cm then use the cutter to cut out 12 circles of dough. Dip the cutter in flour between each cut to stop it sticking. Use a 2cm cutter or the lid of a small bottle to punch out the centre of each round to create the classic ring shape.

4. Fill a medium saucepan with oil, to a depth of around 5cm, and heat until it reaches 190°C on a thermometer. If you don't have a thermometer, test the oil by dropping in a small ball of the doughnut dough. If it sizzles when it makes contact with the oil and takes about 1 minute to brown, the oil is hot enough. Combine the sugar and spices for the coating on a plate, ready to dip the hot doughnuts into. Lay out a double layer of kitchen paper on a baking tray.

5. Fry 2–3 doughnuts at a time, for about 1 minute on each side, until golden brown. Try not to overcrowd the pan or it will lower the temperature of the oil and the doughnuts won't fry properly. Remove the doughnuts from the oil using tongs and drain off the excess oil on the kitchen paper. Fry the 2cm doughnut holes, too. Allow to cool for a minute, then toss the doughnuts and doughnut holes in the spiced sugar ready to eat immediately.

MAKES 12 DOUGHNUTS AND 12 DOUGHNUT HOLES

PREP TIME: 20–25 MINS

COOKING TIME: 12–15 MINS

DOUGHNUTS
75g butter, softened
150g caster sugar
1 egg
400g plain flour, plus extra for dusting
1½ tsp baking powder
½ tsp salt
1 tsp ground cinnamon
½ tsp ground nutmeg
125ml milk
Vegetable oil, for frying

COATING
150g caster sugar
1 tsp ground cinnamon
½ tsp ground nutmeg
½ tsp ground ginger

You will also need a 6cm-round cutter and a 2cm cutter or the lid of a bottle.

Chilli and garlic flatbreads

If you're new to breadmaking, this is a great place to start. These garlic flatbreads are based on a simple bread dough and coated in a hot chilli and garlic butter, and because they only require one rise, you'll be enjoying them before you know it. They are a perfect spicy accompaniment to a barbecue in the summer or warming with a hearty pasta dish in winter – a real all-rounder.

1. Place the flour in a large bowl or the bowl of a stand mixer fitted with the dough-hook attachment, and add the yeast to one side of the bowl and the salt to the other. If you put the salt directly on to the yeast it may kill it, which will stop your dough from rising.

2. Add the olive oil, garlic and 125ml of the water to the bowl and mix until a rough dough forms. Gradually add the rest of the water, mixing until all the flour has been picked up from the sides of the bowl (you might not need all the water, or you might need a little more).

3. Tip the dough on to a lightly floured worktop and knead it by hand (or knead it using the dough hook on the stand mixer) for about 10 minutes or until the dough is smooth and elastic. Lightly grease the bowl in which you mixed the dough with oil, place the dough back into the bowl, cover with a tea towel or cling film and leave to rise at room temperature for 1–3 hours, until doubled in size.

4. While the dough is rising, make the chilli and garlic butter. Melt the butter in a small saucepan and add the chilli (use as much or as little chilli as you like, depending on how hot you want the breads to be) and garlic, and heat over a low heat for a few minutes to gently infuse the butter. Remove from the heat and set to one side.

5. Tip the risen dough out of the bowl on to a lightly floured worktop and fold the dough in on itself a few times to get rid of any irregular air pockets. Divide the dough into 8 pieces and cover with a tea towel to stop the dough drying out.

6. Heat a large dry frying pan over a medium–high heat. Take a piece of dough and roll it out into a large 1cm-thick circle. Brush the top of the dough with some of the infused butter and place the dough butter-side down in the pan. Fry for 2–3 minutes, brush the top with infused butter then flip over and cook until the bread is puffy and has a few golden brown spots. Remove from the pan, brush with more butter and keep warm while you fry the remaining flatbreads. Sprinkle the breads with coriander before serving.

MAKES 8 FLATBREADS

PREP TIME: 25–30 MINS PLUS PROVING TIME

COOKING TIME: 16–24 MINS

GARLIC FLATBREAD
300g strong white bread flour, plus extra for dusting
1 x 7g fast-action dried yeast
1 tsp fine salt
1 tbsp olive oil, plus extra for greasing
1 garlic clove, crushed
175ml water

CHILLI AND GARLIC BUTTER
75g butter
1 small red chilli, deseeded and finely sliced (to taste)
1 garlic clove, crushed
Handful fresh coriander, finely chopped, to serve

Chai tea panna cotta

Panna cotta sounds fancy, but it really couldn't be simpler to make. Chai tea is aromatic and milky, so makes the perfect base for this creamy set dessert. Making a crunchy coconut topping to go with the panna cotta is something I'd really recommend, as the contrasting texture with the silky dessert is a beautiful thing.

1. Place the tea bags in a saucepan with the cinnamon stick, milk, cream and caster sugar. Heat the mixture gently over a low heat, stirring all the time, until the sugar has dissolved. Turn off the heat and allow the tea to infuse for 10 minutes.

2. Put the gelatine leaves in a small bowl, cover with cold water and allow to soften for 5 minutes.

3. Remove the cinnamon stick and tea bags from the infused cream mixture, squeezing the tea bags to extract as much flavour as possible. Strain the mixture through a sieve over a bowl to remove any large bits of cinnamon or tea. Drain the gelatine leaves and squeeze out the excess water, then add the leaves to the warm infused cream mixture and stir until dissolved.

4. Divide the panna cotta mixture evenly among 4 small glasses or teacups. Chill in the fridge for 2–3 hours until set.

5. To make the coconut crumb, preheat the oven to 180°C/160°C fan/gas 4 and line a baking tray with baking parchment. Melt the butter in a small saucepan, then stir in all the dry ingredients. Mix until everything is well combined, then spread the mixture out on the lined baking tray. Bake for 15–20 minutes, using a spoon to break up the mixture halfway through the cooking time, until the crumbs feel dry, then remove from the oven and leave to cool.

6. Sprinkle the cooled coconut crumb around one side of each panna cotta just before serving, then decorate with a few edible flowers for a pop of colour.

MAKES 4 PANNA COTTAS

PREP TIME: 20 MINS PLUS CHILLING TIME

COOKING TIME: 15–20 MINS

PANNA COTTA
2 x chai tea bags
1 cinnamon stick
100ml whole milk
300ml double cream
75g caster sugar
2 sheets leaf gelatine
A few edible flowers,
    to decorate (optional)

COCONUT CRUMB
50g butter
50g desiccated coconut
50g plain flour
50g soft light brown sugar
1 tbsp cocoa powder

Cardamom Knots

Move over cinnamon rolls, this is the new spiced bun on the block. These Swedish buns, also known as Kardemummabullar, are traditionally paired with coffee and served during coffee breaks in Sweden. Cardamom has an amazing slightly spicy, floral and delicately peppery flavour that is underappreciated, but it is shown off properly in these twisted knots. I particularly like these for breakfast to start the day off well. You need ground cardamom for this recipe; lots of supermarkets and health-food shops sell it, but you can also make your own by splitting open green cardamom pods and grinding the small black seeds using a pestle and mortar.

1. Start by making the dough. Place the cubed butter in a small saucepan with the milk. Heat over a low heat until the cubes of butter have completely melted, then remove from the heat and set to one side to allow the mixture to cool for a few minutes.

2. Place the flour in a large bowl, or the bowl of a stand mixer fitted with the dough-hook attachment, and add the yeast to one side of the bowl and the salt, sugar and cardamom to the other. If you put the salt directly on the yeast it may kill it, which will stop your dough from rising.

3. Gradually pour the warm butter and milk into the bowl with the flour, mixing all the time, using your hands or the dough-hook attachment, until a sticky dough forms. You may not need to add all the milk mixture, or you might need to add a little more milk – you want to add just enough to make a sticky but not wet dough.

4. Dust your worktop lightly with flour, tip the dough out on to it and knead it for 5–10 minutes (or knead using the dough hook on the stand mixer) until the dough is no longer sticky and has become smooth and elastic. Grease the bowl in which you mixed the dough with oil, place the dough back in the bowl, cover with a tea towel or cling film and leave to rise at room temperature for 1–3 hours or until doubled in size. You can leave the dough to prove in the fridge overnight if you want these for breakfast!

CONTINUED...

MAKES 12 BUNS

PREP TIME:
45 MINS–1 HOUR
PLUS PROVING TIME

COOKING TIME:
15–20 MINS

DOUGH
50g butter, cubed
250ml whole milk
500g strong white bread flour, plus extra for dusting
1 x 7g sachet fast-action dried yeast
1 tsp fine salt
50g caster sugar
1 tsp ground cardamom
Oil, for greasing

CARDAMOM FILLING
150g butter, softened
100g soft dark brown sugar
2 tsp ground cardamom

CARDAMOM SYRUP
50g caster sugar
½ tsp ground cardamom
Pearl sugar, to decorate (optional)

Cardamom knots

5. While the dough is rising, combine the filling ingredients in a small bowl to make a thick paste. Line 2 baking trays with baking parchment.

6. Tip the risen dough out of the bowl on to a worktop lightly dusted with flour and fold it in on itself a couple of times to knock out any large air pockets.

7. Roll out the dough thinly to make a very large rectangle measuring roughly 50 x 30cm. Spread the cardamom filling mixture all over the dough, making sure it goes right to the edges.

8. Fold one of the short ends over two-thirds of the dough, then fold the remaining third over – as if you are folding a letter or making puff pastry. You should have one neat rectangle consisting of three layers of dough, and all the filling should be enclosed inside.

9. Use a sharp knife to cut the dough into 12 even strips. Taking one of the strips, stretch out and twist it a few times. Tie it into a loose knot, tucking the edges in. Place the knot on a lined baking tray and repeat with the remaining strips, arranging them on the tray and leaving a few centimetres between each. Leave for 45 minutes at room temperature to rise again.

10. While the knots are proving, preheat the oven to 200°C/180°C fan/gas 6. Make the cardamom syrup by bringing the sugar, ground cardamom and 50ml of water to the boil in a small saucepan and letting it bubble for a few minutes, stirring occasionally, until the sugar has dissolved. Remove from the heat.

11. Bake the buns for 15–20 minutes or until golden brown, then brush with the cardamom syrup as soon as they come out of the oven. Sprinkle with pearl sugar, if you wish, and serve warm.

Eggnog layer cake

I've taken all the best elements of eggnog to make this cake as comforting as possible. A hot milk cake soaked in alcoholic syrup, surrounded by a light Italian meringue buttercream and dusted with nutmeg captures the true essence of the drink. Heating the eggs with the sugar over a pan of boiling water makes the cake lighter as the eggs can hold more air when they are whisked, so the resulting structure of the cake is stronger. Italian meringue buttercream is my favourite buttercream because it has a velvety texture but none of the heaviness often associated with the regular variety.

1. Preheat the oven to 180°C/160°C fan/gas 4; grease the base and sides of the cake tins and line them with baking parchment.

2. Start by making the sponge. Heat the butter and milk together in a small saucepan over a low heat until the butter has completely melted and the mixture is beginning to bubble. Remove from the heat and allow to cool to room temperature.

3. Fill a small saucepan about a third full with water and bring to the boil. Have an electric hand-held whisk ready, or fit your stand mixer with the balloon-whisk attachment. In a large heatproof bowl or the bowl of a stand mixer, combine the eggs, caster sugar and vanilla bean paste or extract. Beat the mixture in the bowl over a pan of simmering water using a whisk until the sugar has dissolved. If you rub the mixture between your fingers, you shouldn't feel any grains of sugar. Take the bowl off the heat and whisk on high speed using the electric hand-held whisk or stand mixer for around 10 minutes. The mixture should be really pale and fluffy, and the outside of the bowl should feel slightly warm rather than hot.

4. Sift the flour and baking powder over the whisked egg and sugar, and fold it in using a spatula until combined. Pour the cooled milk and melted butter mixture down the side of the bowl and mix until smooth. Try not to over-mix the batter or you will release the air you whisked in and the cake won't rise as well.

5. Divide the batter evenly between the prepared tins and bake for 35–40 minutes. The cakes should be golden brown and a skewer inserted into the centre should come out clean. Remove from the oven and allow the cakes to cool for 15 minutes in the tin, then turn them out on to a wire rack and leave to cool completely.

SERVES 12–14

PREP TIME: 1–1¼ HOURS PLUS COOLING

COOKING TIME: 35–40 MINS

SPONGE
125g butter
125ml milk
3 large eggs
300g caster sugar
1 tsp vanilla bean paste or
   vanilla extract
175g plain flour
1½ tsp baking powder

BUTTERCREAM
3 large egg whites
175g caster sugar
200g unsalted butter,
   softened and cubed

SYRUP
75g caster sugar
2 tbsp dark rum, brandy
   or bourbon

TO DECORATE
Ground nutmeg
Gold dust

You will also need two 18cm-round cake tins and a sugar thermometer.

6. While the cakes are cooling, make the buttercream. Place the egg whites in a large clean, grease-free bowl or the cleaned bowl from the stand mixer. Combine the sugar and 75ml of water in a small saucepan and set over a medium heat. Stir until the sugar dissolves, then stop stirring and allow the syrup to simmer, placing a sugar thermometer in the pan to monitor the temperature.

7. When the sugar syrup reaches 110°C on the sugar thermometer, start whisking the egg whites on high speed until they form soft peaks. When the syrup reaches 118°C (the soft ball stage), remove it from the heat and slowly pour it down the side of the bowl of the egg whites in a steady stream, whisking all the time. Try to avoid pouring the syrup on to the beaters, as this will create hard sugar crystals. Continue to whisk for 5 minutes, until the meringue is thick and glossy and the outside of the bowl feels cool to the touch.

8. Add the butter, piece by piece, whisking between each addition until all the butter is incorporated and the buttercream is smooth. It is likely that the buttercream will look curdled at some point, but persist with whisking and it will eventually come together. Once all the butter has been incorporated, beat for a further few minutes to make sure the buttercream is really smooth.

9. Make the syrup by combining the sugar and 75ml of water in a small saucepan and bringing to the boil. Stir until the sugar has dissolved, then boil for a further minute before removing from the heat. Stir in your alcohol of choice.

10. Use a serrated knife to cut each cake into two even layers and brush each layer with the alcohol syrup using a pastry brush. Place the bottom layer on a cake stand or cake turntable. Spread with a thin layer of buttercream, then top with the second sponge. Repeat the buttercream process with all the sponge layers before topping with the final layer of sponge. Cover the whole cake with the remaining buttercream using a palette knife, spreading it down the sides to get a smooth finish.

11. Dust the cake with nutmeg and a sprinkle of gold dust, and serve as a dazzling Christmas centrepiece.

Chocolate

Understanding *Chocolate*

There is some scientific evidence regarding why we crave and adore chocolate so. When you allow a piece of chocolate to melt on your tongue, the chemical serotonin is released. This hormone produces feelings of pleasure and happiness, which is why we feel happier after eating chocolate and find it so difficult to stop eating it!

Chocolate is one of those foods people get very passionate about. Whether it's white, dark, milk or all three, I've yet to meet someone who doesn't have a strong opinion on what their favourite is. Arguments extend as far as brands: is it the creamy Cadbury squares or the smooth Galaxy bar of milk chocolate that gets your vote? What percentage of dark chocolate is best? Single or mixed-origin bars?

Chocolate evokes happiness for me – it featured heavily in my childhood. Every time my sister or I got into the car feeling grumpy, my mum would coerce us with a square of chocolate before asking about our day to cheer us up and help us forget about the events of the day. On a Friday night, we'd wait eagerly at the door for my dad to return home from work with 'Friday Chocolate' – an end-of-the-week treat that could be anything from my favourite Aero Mint to bizarre continental chocolates he'd bring home from business abroad.

For a bake that guarantees 'oohs' and 'aahs', anything chocolatey will fit the bill. Whether it be chocolate cookies that ooze molten-chocolate puddles when you break them in two, warm chocolate pudding swimming in sauce, hot chocolate topped with a mountain of whipped cream or fudgy chocolate cake dripping in ganache, it's a winning ingredient.

Melting chocolate

The beauty of chocolate (in its tempered form) is that it melts at just below body temperature. This means that when you place a piece in your mouth it starts melting immediately, releasing its deep chocolatey flavour. It doesn't require harsh heat in order to melt (overheating it can cause it to seize and take on a grainy texture). Melt chocolate gently in a bain marie or in a microwave in short bursts, stirring often. *See*: Gooey Sharing Cookie

Thickens

Cocoa powder can absorb more liquid than its equal weight in flour, which makes it a fantastic thickener – it acts in a similar way to cornflour or arrowroot powder, but has a strong flavour. It is used in cakes, custards and sweets to create structure as well as adding a deep colour and rich chocolatey flavour.
See: Brigadeiros

Water and chocolate

It is commonly said that water and chocolate don't mix. If just a drop of water gets into a bowl of melted chocolate it causes the fat molecules in the chocolate to seize and clump up, making the chocolate unusable. If this happens, don't throw it away! Whisking in a few tablespoons of boiling water will turn your grainy mass into a smooth chocolate sauce, ready to be poured over ice-cream or pancakes.

Cocoa solids

The flavour of chocolate depends heavily on its composition and percentage of cocoa solids. I find dark chocolate with 70% cocoa solids the best to use for baking, as its slightly bitter flavour helps balance the sweetness. Substituting 70% chocolate for one with a higher percentage of cocoa solids will make the finished bake richer and more intense. Milk chocolate is sweeter and can range from 20–45% cocoa solids. Avoid lower-percentage chocolate for baking, as it is overpoweringly sweet and doesn't melt well. *See*: Death by Chocolate Cake

DARK
chocolate
70%

Gooey sharing cookie

Less that 15 minutes to warm molten-chocolate cookie dough? This was my favourite after-school snack growing up, as all it requires are store-cupboard ingredients, and there is virtually no washing up. It's the cookie equivalent of a cake in a mug. You can get creative with this recipe and substitute the chocolate chips for anything that takes your fancy – nuts, dried fruit or toffee pieces make great additions.

1. Preheat the oven to 200°C/180°C fan/gas 6. Have a small ovenproof pan ready.

2. Place the butter in a small heatproof bowl, or in the dish in which you will bake the cookie, and melt it by putting it in the oven for 1–2 minutes or microwaving it in a bowl on High for about 15 seconds. Stir in the soft light brown sugar, golden syrup and vanilla extract.

3. Gently stir the flour and cocoa powder into the butter and sugar mixture, then stir through the chocolate chunks. If your dish is too shallow to mix all the ingredients together easily, you can make the mixture in a small bowl, then press it into the dish or pan once it's mixed. Spread the mixture right into the corners of the dish or pan, smoothing the top to get an even layer of cookie dough. Sprinkle over the salt.

4. Bake for 8–10 minutes or until the top is crisp to the touch and the chocolate has melted. Serve immediately with a scoop of ice-cream or a large glass of cold milk.

MAKES 1 LARGE COOKIE
PREP TIME: 5 MINS
COOKING TIME:
8–10 MINS

50g butter
50g soft light brown sugar
½ tbsp golden syrup
½ tsp vanilla extract
50g self-raising flour
1 tbsp cocoa powder
25g dark chocolate, chopped into small chunks
25g white chocolate, chopped into small chunks
Pinch of sea salt

Lacy pancakes with raspberry sauce

You can create incredible shapes when you drizzle batter into a hot pan – I love how these swirled chocolate treats look. Serve them with whatever takes your fancy. I think chunky raspberry sauce works brilliantly, as the holes in the net bread are the perfect size to scoop up pieces of raspberry.

1. Combine the plain flour, salt and cocoa powder in a medium bowl or jug and make a well in the middle.

2. Pour the beaten egg and half the milk into the centre of the well and whisk until the mixture is smooth and thick. Gradually pour in the rest of the milk, whisking all the time. Transfer the mixture into a squeezy bottle or piping bag.

3. To make the raspberry sauce, place the raspberries, sugar and lemon juice in a small saucepan over a medium heat and cook, stirring all the time, for 5 minutes until the raspberries have broken down to make a thick sauce. Pour into a small heatproof bowl ready to dip.

4. Heat a small amount of oil in a non-stick frying pan. Drizzle the batter into the pan to make a pattern as quickly as you can (the longer you take, the less evenly the pancake will cook). After about 30 seconds, the pancake should have set, so carefully flip it over and briefly cook the other side. Repeat with the remaining batter, keeping the cooked pancakes warm in a low oven.

5. To serve, roll up the pancakes and sprinkle with a little icing sugar before dunking in the raspberry sauce.

MAKES 10 PANCAKES

PREP TIME: 5 MINS

COOKING TIME: 15 MINS

CHOCOLATE BATTER
100g plain flour
½ tsp fine salt
1 tbsp cocoa powder
1 egg, beaten
200ml milk
Vegetable oil, for frying
Icing sugar, for dusting

RASPBERRY SAUCE
100g raspberries, fresh or frozen
1 tbsp caster sugar
1 tbsp lemon juice

You will also need a piping bag or squeezy bottle.

Mint chocolate mousses

I love the sensation of refreshing peppermint cutting through rich chocolate and always add a little peppermint extract to hot chocolate in the winter. This mousse is no exception, with the mint elevating it to a beautiful, light dessert. I use marshmallows to set the mousse instead of gelatine or egg white, which is what makes it so speedy. You can eat it straight after it's spooned into chilled glasses, or it will sit happily in the fridge for a few hours until you're ready to serve.

1. Place 4 glasses (or 8 smaller ramekins or shot glasses) in the freezer on a tray.

2. Put the chopped chocolate, marshmallows, butter and 50ml of water in a medium saucepan over a medium heat and stir occasionally until the mixture is smooth.

3. While the chocolate and marshmallow mixture is melting, whip the cream in a bowl with the peppermint extract, using a manual balloon whisk or an electric hand-held whisk, until it forms soft peaks.

4. When the chocolate mixture is smooth and no lumps of marshmallow can be seen, remove it from the heat. Fold the peppermint cream into the chocolate mixture until it's a uniform pale colour, then divide among the glasses and serve decorated with a mint leaf and a few cocoa nibs, if using.

MAKES 4
PREP TIME: 5 MINS
COOKING TIME: 10 MINS

100g dark chocolate, finely chopped
75g milk chocolate, finely chopped
125g mini marshmallows
35g butter
225ml double cream
1 tsp peppermint extract
4 mint leaves and cocoa nibs (optional), to serve

Toasted marshmallow flapjacks

Flapjack is a quick bake to which I return time and time again. The chocolate chips in this version become molten pockets studded through the oats, and the marshmallows melt and toast on the top, making this bake like eating little mouthfuls of hot s'mores.

MAKES 24 SQUARES OR BARS

PREP TIME: 5 MINS

COOKING TIME: 10–12 MINS

1. Preheat the oven to 200°C/180°C fan/gas 6; grease the baking tray and line it with baking parchment.

2. Place the butter, sugar and golden syrup in a large heavy-based saucepan. Heat the mixture over a medium heat, stirring occasionally, until the butter has completely melted and the sugar has almost dissolved. Remove the pan from the heat.

3. Mix the oats into the hot sugar and butter mixture, and stir together until all the oats are completely coated. Add the marshmallows and unmelted whole chocolate chips, and stir again.

4. Turn the mixture out into the baking tray and use the back of a spatula to press it down into an even layer. Bake for 10–12 minutes, until the marshmallows have started to toast and the flapjack is golden brown. Remove from the oven and leave to cool for a few minutes in the tin, then drizzle with the melted chocolate and use a sharp knife to mark it into 24 bars or squares (while it's still in the tin). The flapjacks will keep in an airtight container for up to 10 days.

125g butter, plus extra for greasing
150g light brown muscovado sugar
1 tbsp golden syrup
225g rolled oats
50g mini marshmallows
50g dark chocolate chips
50g dark chocolate, melted, to drizzle

You will also need a 20 x 30cm baking tray.

EXPRESS

Making mini bites from this flapjack mix will reduce the baking time, meaning you can be enjoying it even faster. Preheat the oven to 200°C/180°C fan/gas 6. Grease a 24-hole mini muffin tin, then fill each hole with 3 teaspoonfuls of the flapjack mixture. Bake for 5–7 minutes.

Brigadeiros

Three ingredients and three simple steps make these sweets a quick and easy gift you can make for someone! Brigadeiros are Brazilian chocolate-fudge truffles, which are often shared to remember happy times and are eaten at all kinds of celebrations. They are not as messy to make as traditional truffles as the chocolates do not melt in your palm! You can roll them in whatever you like: sprinkles are traditional, but I also love the taste of chopped nuts. Pistachios work really well, too.

1. Grease a baking tray with butter.

2. Empty the tin of condensed milk into a large heavy-based saucepan and add the butter. Sift over the cocoa powder and stir briefly with a spatula.

3. Place the pan over a medium heat (not too high or the mixture will catch on the bottom of the pan). Cook the mixture, stirring constantly, for 10 minutes, making sure you scrape the bottom of the pan with a silicone spatula as you stir so that it doesn't stick. When the mixture is ready, it should be very thick and glossy, and when you drop a spoonful of the mixture back into the saucepan it should hold its shape for a few seconds. Pour the Brigadeiros mixture into the buttered baking tray or over a large plate and spread it out thinly before placing in the fridge to cool completely. This should take about 30 minutes if you've spread it thinly.

4. When the mixture is set and cool enough to handle, grease your fingers with butter, take pieces of the mixture and roll them into small balls. You should be able to make 30–35 Brigadeiros. Roll the balls in chocolate sprinkles or chopped nuts before placing in mini paper cases. These sweets will keep well for a few weeks in an airtight container; so they make perfect gifts.

MAKES ABOUT 30–35 BRIGADEIROS

PREP TIME: 15 MINS PLUS COOLING

COOKING TIME: 10 MINS

1 x 397g tin condensed milk
25g butter, plus extra for greasing
25g cocoa powder
Chocolate sprinkles or chopped nuts

You will also need 30–35 mini paper cases.

Chocolate crackle cookies

These taste a little like a cross between a brownie and a cookie, which is never a bad thing in my eyes. Rolling the cookie dough in icing sugar is so simple but creates stunning results. These are best eaten warm, dunked into a cold glass of milk as an afternoon snack.

MAKES ABOUT 30 COOKIES

PREP TIME: 10 MINS PLUS CHILLING

COOKING TIME: 7–9 MINS

100g butter, softened
100g caster sugar
100g soft dark brown sugar
1 egg
125g plain flour
50g cocoa powder
½ tsp bicarbonate of soda
100g icing sugar

1. Cream the butter, caster sugar and brown sugar together in a large bowl using an electric hand-held whisk or in a stand mixer until really pale and fluffy. Add the egg and whisk again to combine.

2. In a separate bowl, mix together the flour, cocoa powder and bicarbonate of soda. Fold the dry ingredients into the butter and sugar mixture and beat until really well combined. The mixture should be thick and hold together well. Place the bowl of dough in the fridge to firm up for at least 1 hour (or freeze it for 30 minutes if you're short of time).

3. While the cookie dough is chilling, preheat the oven to 180°C/160°C fan/gas 4 and line a baking sheet with baking parchment. Tip the icing sugar into a medium bowl.

4. Using a teaspoon to scoop and your hands to mould, make about 30 small balls from the chilled dough, then roll the balls in the icing sugar, making sure they are completely covered in sugar. Place the sugar-coated balls on the baking sheet, leaving plenty of space between each one for them to spread out.

5. Bake the cookies for 7–9 minutes until spread out and cracked but still very soft and puffy in the middle. Allow them to cool briefly on the tray – the middles will sink down, making the centres beautifully soft. Enjoy slightly warm for the best experience!

EXPRESS

Make this recipe up to step 4 but don't roll the balls in icing sugar just yet. Freeze the cookie dough balls in a suitable container or zip-lock bag, and when you crave one or two warm cookies, simply roll in icing sugar and pop them into the oven at 180°C/160°C fan/gas 4 for 9–11 minutes.

Self-saucing chocolate pudding

I made my first self-saucing pudding on a rainy afternoon back when I was around 12 years old. I was immediately captivated by the magic transformation that happens when you put a peculiar-looking dessert, swimming in too much liquid, into the oven and walk away feeling bemused. Just 30 minutes later, you return to open the oven door and reveal a perfectly risen pud, concealing a thick chocolate sauce when you dig right to the bottom of the dish. Using coffee in the pouring liquid intensifies the flavour of the chocolate, which can never be a bad thing.

1. Preheat the oven to 180°C/160°C fan/gas 4 and grease the baking dish with butter.

2. Combine the flour, caster sugar, 30g cocoa powder and baking powder in a large bowl.

3. Melt the butter in the microwave or a small saucepan and beat together the milk and eggs in a small jug. Add the melted butter to the jug, then pour the wet ingredients into the dry ingredients. Fold through the chocolate chips and spread the mixture into the baking dish.

4. Mix the muscovado sugar with the remaining tablespoon of cocoa powder in a bowl and stir in the coffee or boiling water, then pour this mixture over the cake batter. This feels like a very odd thing to do, but the liquid will soak through the cake as it bakes, making it deliciously moist, and create the sauce at the bottom.

5. Bake for 30 minutes until the cake is risen and firm. A rich, glossy sauce should have formed underneath, so serve the pudding immediately to stop the sauce from soaking back into the sponge. Serve with a handful of fresh berries or a few scoops of passionfruit seeds to cut through the richness.

SERVES 6

PREPARATION TIME: 20 MINS

COOKING TIME: 30 MINS

175g self-raising flour
100g caster sugar
30g cocoa powder, plus 1 tbsp
½ tsp baking powder
75g butter, plus extra for greasing
150ml milk
2 eggs
75g dark chocolate chips
150g light brown muscovado sugar
200ml freshly brewed coffee (or boiling water)
Fresh berries or passionfruit seeds, to serve

You will also need a 1.5 litre baking dish.

Earl Grey, caramel and chocolate loaf cake

Why have a cup of tea and a slice of cake when you can have both together? Aromatic Earl Grey tea is infused into every part of this cake. It elevates what could be a bold and brash slab of cake into something delicate and refined, with the tea creating a refreshing backdrop. I like to sprinkle loose-leaf tea over the top of the cake as the vibrant blue cornflowers pop against the creamy caramel.

1. Preheat the oven to 180°C/160°C fan/gas 4, then grease the loaf tin and line it with baking parchment.

2. Place the Earl Grey teabags for the sponge in a mug or small heatproof jug and pour 150ml of boiling water over the top. Leave to brew for 5 minutes.

3. While the tea is brewing, combine the plain flour, both sugars, cocoa powder and bicarbonate of soda in a large bowl.

4. Melt the butter in a bowl in the microwave or a small saucepan and remove the teabags from the tea, discarding the teabags. Whisk the yoghurt, egg and brewed tea into the melted butter.

5. Pour the wet mixture into the dry ingredients, whisking until a smooth batter has formed. It will be fairly runny but don't worry – this is normal. Scrape the batter into the loaf tin and bake for 35–40 minutes or until risen, and a skewer inserted into the centre comes out clean.

6. While the cake is baking, make the caramel sauce. Gently heat the cream in a small saucepan with the Earl Grey teabag until the cream is steaming and slightly coloured by the tea. Pour it into a small heatproof jug and set aside to infuse for 5 minutes, then squeeze out the teabag and discard.

7. Make the Salted Caramel Sauce on page 152, using the infused cream instead of the regular cream. Allow the sauce to cool briefly before using.

8. Remove the cake from the oven and let it cool for 10 minutes in the tin, then carefully remove it and transfer it to a wire rack. Pour over the caramel sauce and leave it to set briefly before sprinkling with loose-leaf Earl Grey (if using), slicing and enjoying.

MAKES 1 LOAF CAKE

PREP TIME: 20-25 MINS PLUS COOLING

COOKING TIME: 35-40 MINS

SPONGE
3 Earl Grey teabags
125g plain flour
125g caster sugar
100g soft light brown sugar
50g cocoa powder
1 tsp bicarbonate of soda
60g butter, plus extra for greasing
125g natural yoghurt
1 egg

EARL GREY CARAMEL SAUCE
125ml double cream
1 Earl Grey teabag
1 quantity of Salted Caramel Sauce (see page 152) made with Earl Grey-infused cream
Loose-leaf Earl Grey (with the blue flowers, if possible), to decorate (optional)

You will also need a 500g loaf tin.

Mississippi mud pie

If an intensely chocolatey dessert is what you are after, you won't find one more satisfying than this. The four layers meld together beautifully, providing a great amalgamation of textures – smooth chocolate pudding, fudgy cake and a mountain of whipped cream, all piled into a dark, buttery case. To make this incredibly indulgent chocolate pudding gluten free, simply swap the chocolate biscuits for your favourite gluten-free alternative.

1. Preheat the oven to 200°C/180°C fan/gas 6 and grease the cake tin with butter.

2. Start by making the base. Blitz the biscuits in a food processor until they form fine crumbs. Alternatively, place them in a large plastic bag, seal and bash them with a rolling pin. Transfer the crushed biscuits to a bowl. Melt the butter in a small saucepan or in a bowl in the microwave, pour it into the bowl of biscuit crumbs and stir through until well coated. Press the crumbs into the cake tin using your hands, pushing the mixture about 5cm up the sides of the tin. Use the back of a spoon to make sure the base is firmly pressed into the tin, then chill until needed.

3. To make the fudge cake layer, whisk the soft brown sugar with the eggs in a bowl using an electric hand-held whisk for about 5 minutes until very thick and pale, then whisk in the vanilla. Place the golden syrup, dark chocolate and butter in a heatproof bowl set over a pan of simmering water until melted. Fold the chocolate mixture into the whisked eggs and sugar until well combined, then pour it over the chilled base. Bake for 25–30 minutes until a crust has formed but the centre retains a slight wobble, then remove from the oven and allow to cool completely before returning it to the fridge.

4. While the fudge cake layer is baking, make the chocolate pudding. Combine the cornflour, sugar and salt in a medium saucepan and slowly whisk in the milk in a slow and steady stream, stirring all the time so lumps don't form. Cook over a medium heat, stirring occasionally with a spatula, for about 10 minutes. Use a whisk if lumps start to form. When the mixture is thick enough to coat the back of a spoon and has a custard-like consistency, add the chocolate and continue stirring for another 2–3 minutes until the mixture is quite thick. If there are any lumps in the mixture, push it through a sieve to remove them. Pour the mixture into a glass bowl and cover with a sheet of cling film, then transfer to the fridge to cool completely.

SERVES 12

PREP TIME: 50 MINS PLUS COOLING

COOKING TIME: 25–30 MINS

BASE
300g Oreo cookies or other chocolate sandwich biscuits
75g butter, plus extra for greasing

FLOURLESS FUDGE CAKE LAYER
150g soft light brown sugar
3 eggs
1 tsp vanilla extract or vanilla bean paste
3 tbsp golden syrup
125g dark chocolate, chopped
75g butter

CHOCOLATE PUDDING
2 tbsp cornflour
100g caster sugar
1 tsp salt
500ml whole milk
175g dark chocolate, chopped

TOPPING
300ml double cream
Cocoa powder and chocolate shavings, to decorate

5. Whisk the cream for the topping in a bowl until it forms soft peaks. Pour the chocolate pudding mixture on top of the base and fudge cake, then spoon the cream over the top of that. Dust with cocoa powder, sprinkle over chocolate shavings, then return to the fridge until ready to serve. This pie will keep in the fridge for up to 4 days.

You will also need a 23cm loose-bottomed cake tin.

Triple chocolate éclairs

When a plain chocolate éclair doesn't quite cut it, these are a step up. Fancy éclairs are very popular in London, but fancy doesn't have to mean they aren't decadent! Silky chocolate crème pâtissière isn't as difficult to make as it sounds and tastes unbelievably good combined with crisp cocoa choux and sticky chocolate glaze. You can make these in a miniature form for an afternoon tea, too.

1. Preheat the oven to 180°C/160°C fan/gas 4 and line 2 large baking sheets with baking parchment.

2. To make the choux pastry, place the butter, sugar and 125ml of water in a small saucepan over a medium–high heat. Bring the mixture to a rolling boil and when all the butter has melted, keeping the pan on the heat, add the flour and cocoa powder, and vigorously beat the mixture with a wooden spoon until a smooth ball of dough forms.

3. Continue to cook the dough for a further minute, stirring rapidly and continuously. Tip the dough out into a bowl and leave it to cool until it has stopped steaming. If the dough hasn't cooled properly when you add the eggs, they will scramble.

4. Beat the eggs together briefly in a small jug. Add the eggs to the cooled dough in three separate additions, beating well between each one with a spatula or an electric hand-held whisk. It can be quite difficult to work in, but keep mixing and it will turn into a thick paste. You might not need to add all the egg, so add the final amount slowly. Your mixture should fall off a spatula easily and leave a 'V' shape. Spoon the choux pastry into one of the piping bags.

5. Line up a ruler next to the baking sheets and pipe 12 x 10cm éclairs on to the lined baking sheets, leaving plenty of space between each one to allow for them to expand as they cook. Use a wet finger to smooth over any lumps. Bake for 25–30 minutes or until the choux feels crisp and hollow. Keep a close eye on them as the dark colour makes it difficult to see how well baked they are. When they are cooked through, turn the oven off and leave the éclair shells in the cooling oven to dry out.

MAKES 12 ÉCLAIRS

PREP TIME: 45 MINS PLUS COOLING

COOKING TIME: 25–30 MINS

CHOCOLATE CHOUX PASTRY

75g butter, diced

1 tsp caster sugar

70g strong white bread flour

30g cocoa powder

3 eggs

CRÈME PÂTISSIÈRE FILLING

4 egg yolks

100g caster sugar

4 tbsp cornflour

500ml whole milk

75g dark chocolate, finely chopped

25g butter

CHOCOLATE GLAZE

100g dark chocolate, chopped

100ml double cream

TO DECORATE

50g white chocolate

You will also need 2 piping bags fitted with large open-star nozzles.

6. To make the chocolate crème pâtissière, place the egg yolks, sugar and cornflour in a large heatproof jug and whisk until combined and slightly paler in colour. Heat the milk in a large saucepan over a medium heat until steaming. Gradually pour the hot milk into the egg mixture, whisking all the time until the mixture is smooth.

7. Transfer the mixture back into the saucepan and heat gently for a few minutes, whisking all the time, until the custard is thick and smooth. Remove from the heat and stir in the chopped chocolate and the butter. When they are completely melted and no lumps remain, pour the mixture into a bowl, cover with cling film and chill until completely cool and ready to use.

8. To make the chocolate glaze, place the chopped dark chocolate in a small heatproof bowl. Heat the cream in a small saucepan until steaming, then pour it over the chocolate and stir together until all the chocolate has melted. Melt the white chocolate for the decoration in the microwave or in a heatproof bowl over a pan of gently simmering water.

9. Slice each cooled éclair in half lengthways using a serrated knife. Dip the top half into the chocolate glaze, then spoon the chilled chocolate crème pâtissière into the second piping bag and pipe it into the bottom half of each éclair. Top with a glazed half, then drizzle with melted white chocolate.

EXPRESS

Make dainty mini éclairs for an afternoon tea or smaller snack! Make the choux dough as above, piping 24 x 5cm lengths instead of 10cm éclairs. Bake for 20–25 minutes or until crisp and hollow, then prepare in the same way as above. You can also make the shells in advance and freeze them, defrosting 15 minutes before ready to fill.

Caramelised white chocolate cake

Caramelised white chocolate was a complete revelation to me. A process as simple as baking transforms ordinary chunks of white chocolate into a glossy, caramel-flavoured pool that is reminiscent of the Caramac bars my parents loved from their childhood. Make a big batch of the caramelised chocolate and use it in everything: drizzle it over ice-cream, pour it on to warm brownies or eat by the spoon.

1. Preheat the oven to 140°C/120°C fan/gas 1. Place the chopped chocolate in a non-stick baking tin (a brownie or traybake tin works perfectly) and bake for 10 minutes.

2. Remove the tin from the oven and use a spatula to give the chocolate a good stir. Return the tin to the oven and bake for a further 1–1½ hours, removing and stirring the chocolate every 15 minutes. As the cooking progresses the chocolate will change in texture and colour, occasionally appearing lumpy and grainy. Don't panic about this – as the chocolate caramelises it will become smooth. When the chocolate is a golden-brown colour and smells caramel-like, remove the tin from the oven, pour the chocolate into a small heatproof bowl and leave to cool.

3. Turn the oven up to 180°C/160°C fan/gas 4. Line the base of the cake tins with baking parchment and grease the sides with butter.

4. Melt the butter for the sponge in a small saucepan and heat until completely melted. Continue to cook the butter over a medium heat until it starts to foam and smell nutty, then remove from the heat. Some of the solids in the butter will have turned a light brown colour.

5. Put the eggs and sugar in a large bowl or the bowl of a stand mixer and whisk using an electric hand-held whisk or whisk attachment for 7–10 minutes until tripled in volume.

6. When the mixture is very pale and thick enough to hold a trail when the beaters are lifted out, carefully sift over the flour. Gently fold the flour into the mixture using a spatula, taking care not to knock out too much of the air you've just incorporated. Make sure you scoop right down to the bottom of the bowl so that all the flour gets mixed in. Drizzle the browned butter, including the solids from the bottom of the pan, around the edges of the bowl and gently stir in until just incorporated, then divide the mixture evenly between the two tins.

MAKES 1 LARGE CAKE

PREP TIME: 1 HOUR

COOKING TIME: 1–1½ HOURS FOR THE CARAMELISED CHOCOLATE PLUS 20–25 MINS FOR THE CAKE

CARAMELISED WHITE CHOCOLATE
200g good-quality white chocolate, chopped

SPONGE
50g butter, plus extra for greasing
6 eggs
200g caster sugar
200g plain flour

BUTTERCREAM
125g unsalted butter, softened
125g icing sugar
100g caramelised white chocolate (as above)

GANACHE
50ml double cream
100g caramelised white chocolate (as above)

7. Bake the sponges for 20–25 minutes, until the cakes are golden and shrinking away from the edges of the tin. Remove from the oven and leave to cool for 10 minutes in the tins, then transfer to a wire rack and allow to cool completely.

8. To make the buttercream, beat the butter and icing sugar together in a stand mixer fitted with a paddle attachment or in a bowl using an electric hand-held whisk for up to 10 minutes, until the mixture is very pale (almost white) and fluffy. Pour in half of the melted caramelised white chocolate and whisk for a few more minutes. If the chocolate has solidified, pop it back into the oven on a very low heat to melt again.

9. To make the ganache, heat the cream in a small saucepan until steaming, then pour over the remaining melted caramelised white chocolate. Stir together to make a smooth ganache, then spoon into the piping bag.

10. When the sponges are completely cold, place one of them on a cake stand or serving plate and top with half the buttercream. Drizzle half of the ganache over the buttercream, then top with the other sponge. Swirl the remaining buttercream on the top of the cake and finish with a drizzled swirl of ganache.

You will also need 2 x 20cm-round cake tins and a disposable piping bag (optional).

Death by chocolate cake

Of all the ways to go, death by chocolate cake sounds like one of the best! When you're desperate for a chocolate fix, this is the cake for you. Dangerously decadent, it features two different types of chocolate, a dense, fudgy layer of dark chocolate sponge, whipped chocolate ganache and a chocolate drizzle. Top that off with even more chocolate curls and you've created a cake that people dream of. The different types of chocolate work harmoniously, resulting in a cake that isn't too sweet or too rich. You'll make this cake again and again – it's my most requested birthday cake!

1. Preheat the oven to 180°C/160°C fan/gas 4, then grease the cake tins and line them with baking parchment.

2. Place the flour, caster sugar, cocoa powder, bicarbonate of soda and salt in a large bowl and stir together.

3. Melt the chocolate and butter together in a heatproof bowl in the microwave or set over a pan of simmering water. When they are fully melted and no lumps remain, whisk in the buttermilk, coffee and eggs.

4. Pour the wet mixture into the dry ingredients, whisking until a smooth, runny batter has formed. Divide the mixture evenly between the three prepared tins, either by counting equal spoonfuls of mixture or by weighing the tins. Bake the three cakes for 25–30 minutes until risen and a skewer inserted into the centre comes out clean. Remove from the oven and leave to cool in the tins for 10 minutes, then transfer to a wire rack to cool completely.

5. To make the ganache, place the butter, chocolate and golden syrup in a heatproof bowl over a pan of simmering water. Stir until the mixture is melted and smooth. Remove from the heat and pour in the double cream, then mix until combined. Place in the fridge and chill for 30 minutes until cool but not set firm.

6. Whip the cooled ganache with an electric hand-held whisk for 2–3 minutes until it turns from dark to pale brown. Use a spatula to scrape down the sides of the bowl during the whisking to make sure all the ganache is properly whipped.

MAKES 1 LARGE CELEBRATION CAKE

PREPARATION TIME: 1–1¼ HOURS PLUS COOLING

COOKING TIME: 25–30 MINS

SPONGE
250g plain flour
250g caster sugar
75g cocoa powder
2 tsp bicarbonate of soda
½ tsp salt
100g dark chocolate, chopped
125g butter, plus extra for greasing
250ml buttermilk (or 245ml whole milk plus 1 tbsp lemon juice)
250ml strong-brewed coffee
2 eggs

WHIPPED CHOCOLATE GANACHE
150g butter, cubed
150g milk chocolate, chopped
150g dark chocolate, chopped
2 tbsp golden syrup
300ml double cream

CHOCOLATE

7. When the sponges are completely cool, assemble the cake. Put a small blob of the ganache on a cake stand or serving plate (use a cake turntable if you have one) and place the first layer of sponge on top of it. This will secure the cake and stop it sliding while you decorate it. Spread the first layer of sponge with quarter of the ganache using a palette knife, then top with the second layer of sponge. Repeat the process with the next layer of sponge, then cover the whole cake with a thin layer of ganache, reserving most for later. This is called the crumb coat, which stops crumbs spreading into the outer icing. Place the cake in the fridge for 15 minutes for the ganache to set.

8. When the cake has been chilled, completely cover the cake with most of the remaining ganache. Use a large palette knife to create smooth edges by holding it vertically at a 90° angle to the cake and running it all the way around. When you're happy with the appearance, return the cake to the fridge for 30 minutes to firm up. Spoon the last of the whipped ganache into the piping bag fitted with the closed-star nozzle.

9. To make the ganache drip, put the finely chopped dark chocolate in a small heatproof jug. Heat the double cream in a small saucepan until it is steaming, then pour it over the chocolate and stir until all the chocolate has melted. Set to one side to thicken slightly – you want it to be firm enough to hold its shape on the cake but runny enough to drip. Make chocolate curls by running a sharp knife over the back of the chocolate bar.

10. Remove the cake from the fridge. Pipe small swirls of whipped ganache around the top edge of the cake. Spoon the runnier ganache drip into the second piping bag, snip off the end and pipe a border around the top edge of the cake, allowing it to run down the sides to create drips that run halfway down the cake. Pipe the remaining runny ganache on to the centre of the cake and spread it gently so that it covers it evenly in one single layer. Allow to firm up for a few minutes, then top with a few chocolate curls cut from the bar of dark chocolate.

GANACHE DRIP
100g dark chocolate,
 finely chopped
75ml double cream
1 small bar dark chocolate,
 to decorate

You will also need 3 x 18cm-round cake tins and 2 disposable piping bags, one fitted with a open-star nozzle.

Mocha cruffins

I love hybrid bakes! Why just have one sweet treat when you can have two rolled into one? Cruffins are my favourite, because they have all the buttery flakiness of a croissant packed into a neat muffin shape that is acceptable as an afternoon snack. I'm a big advocate of all-day croissant eating – especially when they're dripping in mocha glaze and have a hidden cocoa swirl in the centre.

1. Place both the flours, the sugar and 100g of the butter in the bowl of a food processor. Add the yeast to one side of the bowl and salt to the other side. Pulse once or twice, until the butter is coated in flour but is still in fairly large lumps. You need to be able to see chunks of butter or the dough won't puff when it is baked. Alternatively, mix the ingredients by hand in a large bowl, taking care not to rub in the butter too much.

2. Remove the bowl from the processor, if using, and take out the blade, then gradually pour in the water and milk. Gently mix with a spoon until a loose dough forms. You might need to add a few more drops of water to mop up any excess flour. Shape the dough into a rectangle, wrap it in cling film and place in the fridge for 1 hour. Wrap the remaining butter in cling film and place it in the freezer to chill.

3. Lightly flour a clean worktop and tip the chilled dough out on to it. Roll it out into a large rectangle three times as long as it is wide and grate the frozen butter over the top two-thirds. Fold the bottom third up over the middle third, and then fold the top third down over that, as if you were folding a letter. Wrap the dough in cling film and chill in the fridge for 20 minutes.

4. Remove the dough from the fridge and place it so the short open end is facing you. Roll the dough out into a rectangle and repeat the folding process again, ending with wrapping and chilling the dough for 20 minutes. Repeat twice more, so the dough is folded into three a total of 4 times.

5. Roll the dough out into a 20 x 40cm rectangle. Trim the edges with a sharp knife to help achieve the best puff. Combine the cocoa powder and espresso powder in a small container and sift it over the dough, using the back of a spoon to help it bond. Roll the dough up tightly, starting at the long side, then wrap in cling film and return to the fridge for 20 minutes.

6. Slice the cruffin log into 8 pieces and nestle each one into the holes of a muffin tin. Cover with a sheet of oiled cling film and leave to prove at room temperature for 20–30 minutes.

MAKES 8 CRUFFINS

PREP TIME: 45–50 MINS, PLUS AT LEAST 3¼ HOURS CHILLING AND PROVING TIME

COOKING TIME: 20–25 MINS

CRUFFIN
100g plain flour, plus extra for dusting
150g strong white flour
30g caster sugar, plus extra for coating
200g cold unsalted butter, diced
7g sachet fast-action dried yeast
½ tsp fine salt
50ml water
75ml whole milk, at room temperature
1 tbsp cocoa powder
2 tsp espresso powder

GLAZE
100g icing sugar
1 tsp cocoa powder
½ tsp espresso powder
1 tbsp milk

You will also need a 12-hole muffin tin.

7. Preheat the oven to 200°C/180°C fan/gas 6. Bake the cruffins in the centre of the oven for 20–25 minutes or until they are dark golden brown.

8. While the cruffins are baking, make the glaze. Sift the icing sugar, cocoa powder and espresso powder together in a small bowl, then add the milk and mix thoroughly to form a thick paste.

9. When the cruffins are baked, leave them to cool in the tin for 5 minutes, then roll in caster sugar to coat and spread the glaze on the top while they are still warm. It should drip down into the cruffin, infusing the mocha flavour all the way through.

Caramel

Understanding *Caramel*

Caramel is kitchen alchemy. The finished product is worth so much more than the sum of its parts; simple white sugar melts into pools of liquid gold with the application of heat. It can be made even more lustrous and glossy with the addition of cream, butter and salt. It's the definition of indulgence, and if I'm not baking with it you'll probably find me eating caramel sauce with a spoon.

There were two things I was banned from doing in the kitchen when I was a child: deep-fat frying and making caramel. I can see the sense in the rule, as both require extremely high temperatures and are fairly dangerous, but I was aching to make my own caramel. As an 11-year-old, I'd stop at the local corner shop and spend my pocket money on a 10p bar of chocolate-covered caramel. I'd leave it in my coat pocket so that it would harden in the cold into an even chewier stick of deliciousness, the chocolate cracking when you sink your teeth in. Chewy toffees are always the first to disappear from Christmas boxes of chocolate in my house. No one in our family can resist that jaw-sticking sweet that clings to your teeth in a sugary mass – it's guaranteed to generate a few minutes of peace and quiet.

Salted caramel has taken the world by storm, with people embracing it as a welcome new friend, although some have rejected it as a fad that will blow over. I side with the first group, as I believe that most people adore sweet and salty flavours together, even if they don't realise it. Hot buttered toast with jam or honey, pancakes with maple syrup and bacon or even simple butter toffees are all flying the sweet-and-salty flag. A little salt is needed to offset the extreme sweetness in caramel-based bakes, so don't leave it out.

Flavour

Caster or granulated sugar taste of
little besides sweetness. However,
melting it and heating it causes the
sugar molecules to break apart and
react with each other, creating
new compounds with complex
aromas and giving it a golden-
brown colour. When you smell and
taste caramel, you should detect
buttery, bitter, nutty and malty
notes. *See:* Salted Caramel Sauce

Caramelising

Making caramel is a straightforward process, but
the temperature needs to be carefully controlled
– a sugar thermometer is essential and a heavy-
based pan ideal, as it heats the sugar more evenly.
Caramelisation starts at around 160°C, when sugar
begins to melt. At 175°C it becomes pale brown
and, if allowed to cool and harden, will be glass-like
and perfect for decorations or to use as an edible
glue. If you continue heating it, it darkens as the
temperature increases, progressing from pale brown
to dark amber. The hotter the caramel, the more
bitter it becomes. Once caramel reaches 200°C it
is thought too dark to work with and unusable.
See: Burnt Caramel Banana Bread

Wet or dry?

There are two classic methods for
making caramel: 'wet' (a sugar and
water mix) and 'dry' (sugar alone).
Both deliver the same results. The wet
method takes a little longer, but I find
it easier to control the caramelisation
as the heat is distributed more evenly.
The only drawback is that the caramel
might crystallise if stirred.
 The dry method requires
 more attention to stop
 hot spots from darkening
 too quickly, but can be
 stirred without the
 sugars crystallising.
See: (Wet) Flourless
Hazelnut Torte;
(Dry) Pecan Praline
Brownies

Infusion

Caramels can be
transformed into delicious
sauces and fillings which
can be infused with many
different flavours. Try
adding citrus zest for a zingy
treat, a spoonful of rum for
an alcoholic kick, or herbs
and spices. *See:* Caramel
Madeleines with Buttered
Rum Sauce

Salted caramel sauce

If you're a caramel addict like me, who will drizzle salted caramel on just about anything, you need a great salted caramel sauce recipe under your belt. People are often scared to try making caramel, but it's not as hard as you might think. When you are bubbling the sugar and water, you'll smell when the sugar starts to turn from sugary water and caramelise into an almost bitter-smelling caramel. As soon as you detect the first note of bitterness, remove the caramel from the heat and add the other ingredients.

MAKES 1 LARGE JAR
PREP TIME: 5 MINS
COOKING TIME: 6–7 MINS

250g caster sugar
100g butter
125ml double cream
1 tsp flaked sea salt

1. Place the sugar and 100ml of water in a heavy-based saucepan and stir briefly to combine. Set over a medium heat and allow the mixture to bubble for 5–6 minutes until it turns golden brown in colour. Try not to stir the mixture while it caramelises or the sugar might crystallise, but you can swirl the pan occasionally if the caramel is colouring unevenly.

2. When the sugar reaches a dark amber colour and starts to smell caramelised, remove from the heat and stir in the butter. The mixture will splutter and bubble, so be careful.

3. Slowly pour in the double cream, stirring as you add it. Return the mixture to the heat for 1 minute, then stir in the sea salt. Remove from the heat, allow the caramel to cool slightly then taste it to see if you need to add any more salt.

4. Pour the caramel into a large sterilised jar (see page 10 for sterilising method) and keep in the fridge until ready to use. When you want to use the caramel, warm it up for a few seconds in the microwave to return it to a liquid. The sauce will keep in the fridge for up to 1 month.

Hot chocolate with caramel pretzel bites

If you've spent your hot-chocolate-drinking days consuming the instant variety, promise never to do so again. Hot chocolate from scratch is so simple to make and far richer, creamier and more chocolatey! A swirl of salted caramel tempers the chocolate with a sweet undertone. Enjoy with pretzel bites for a salty, chewy crunch on the side.

1. Preheat the oven to 200°C/180°C fan/gas 6 and line a baking sheet with parchment.

2. Sandwich each caramel between 2 pretzels and put on the baking sheet. Bake for 5 minutes or until the caramels have melted, then remove from the oven to cool.

3. Heat the milk in a saucepan over a medium heat. When the milk looks like it is about to boil, remove the pan from the heat and stir in the chopped chocolate and 1 tablespoon of the salted caramel sauce, if using. Leave for 1 minute, for the chocolate to melt, then whisk until smooth and frothy.

4. Drizzle the remaining salted caramel around the rim of 2 heatproof glasses using a spoon or squeezy bottle. Fill with the hot chocolate and top with, if you like, whipped cream, more salted caramel sauce and a pretzel bite. Serve immediately.

MAKES 2 MUGFULS AND 10 PRETZEL BITES

PREP TIME: 10 MINS

COOKING TIME: 5 MINS

PRETZEL BITES
10 chocolate-coated caramels (Rolos are perfect)
20 mini salted pretzels

HOT CHOCOLATE
500ml whole milk
75g dark chocolate, finely chopped
2 tbsp Salted Caramel Sauce (opposite), plus extra to serve (optional)
Whipped cream, to serve (optional)

Brown sugar beignets

Beignets are essentially deep-fried choux buns. They have an irresistible crisp exterior, hiding a soft, caramel-flavoured buttery centre, and are rolled in icing sugar for good measure. I love the rich molasses flavour that dark brown sugar brings to these sweet snacks but you could use light brown sugar if you prefer a milder flavour.

1. Place the butter and 100ml of water in a small saucepan and bring to the boil. When the butter has melted and the mixture is bubbling, add the sugar to the pan and stir to dissolve. Beat in the flour until a smooth and thick dough forms, then continue to cook the dough for a further minute before removing from the heat and tipping it into a heatproof bowl to cool briefly.

2. While the dough is cooling, pour the oil into a saucepan and heat over a medium heat until it reaches 180°C (or until it sizzles when you drop in a small piece of the dough). Your mixture should fall off a spatula easily and leave a 'V' shape (you might not need all the egg).

3. When the dough has cooled slightly, beat in the eggs a little at a time until the dough is smooth.

4. Use 2 teaspoons together to form small balls or quenelles of the dough, then drop them into the hot oil, a few at a time. Fry for 2–3 minutes until golden brown all over, then drain the cooked beignets on a few sheets of kitchen paper. Toss in icing sugar and serve hot. Repeat with the rest of the dough.

EXPRESS

Make the beignet batter up to step 4 then cover the bowl with cling film or a lid and chill for up to 3 days. Heat the oil and fry the beignets following the instructions in step 4, when you want to eat them.

MAKES 30 BEIGNETS
PREP TIME: 10 MINS
COOKING TIME:
10 MINS

50g butter, cubed
50g soft dark brown sugar
75g plain flour
1 litre vegetable oil, for
    frying
2 eggs, beaten
Icing sugar, to dust

Honeycomb cups

I love big, bold shards of glittering honeycomb dunked in chocolate, but these cups possess all the right flavours in a more contained form and don't turn sticky as quickly as broken honeycomb. You have to work quickly to fill the cups before the honeycomb sets, so make sure you grease the tin well first. These make great snacks or canapés for a party.

1. Grease 8 holes of the muffin tin liberally with butter and set to one side. The cups will get stuck if the holes are not really well greased.

2. Stir together the caster sugar and golden syrup in a deep, heavy-based saucepan. Once combined, stop stirring and heat over a medium–high heat for about 5 minutes, allowing the mixture to bubble until it is a deep amber colour and has a caramelised aroma.

3. Remove from the heat and rapidly whisk in the bicarbonate of soda. The mixture will bubble up as the bicarbonate of soda reacts with the sugar. It will rise and fall as it foams, but keep mixing for about 20 seconds so the mixture settles slightly and won't swell in the cups. Divide the hot sugar among the 8 greased muffin tin holes, working as quickly as you can so that the bubbles don't completely deflate. Allow the cups to harden completely in the tin before removing.

4. Heat the cream in a small saucepan until it is steaming but not boiling. Place the chocolate in a small heatproof bowl, pour the hot cream over the chocolate and leave to stand for 1 minute before stirring until smooth. Whisk with an electric hand-held whisk until thick, then spoon into the piping bag. Pipe a swirl on to the top of each honeycomb cup and eat as soon as possible, as the ganache can make the honeycomb sticky.

MAKES 8 CUPS

PREP TIME: 5–10 MINS
PLUS COOLING

COOKING TIME: 5 MINS

Butter, for greasing
100g caster sugar
2 tbsp golden syrup
1 tsp bicarbonate of soda
100ml double cream
100g milk chocolate,
    chopped

You will also need a
12-hole muffin tin and a
piping bag fitted with a
closed-star nozzle.

Salted caramel cornflake bars

Everyone loves sweet treats made with cornflakes. You take this well-known and plain cereal and turn it into something so moreish and delicious – a far cry from a sad-looking breakfast option. These bars are my secret weapon for bake-sales (especially when you forget to make anything and find yourself baking at midnight), and no one needs to know how easy they are.

1. Grease and line the tin with baking parchment. Even though the bars aren't going to be baked, greasing the tin with butter helps the parchment stick.

2. Place the butter in a large saucepan, add both sugars and the mini marshmallows, and place the pan over a medium heat.

3. Allow the mixture to bubble, stirring often, until the marshmallows have completely melted and the mixture is smooth. Remove from the heat and stir in the vanilla and salt.

4. Add the cornflakes to the saucepan and mix gently until they are fully coated in the caramel mixture. Don't be afraid to crush the cornflakes with the spoon, as any smaller pieces help the bars to stick together.

5. Spread the mixture out into the lined tin, gently pushing it right into the corners using a spatula, then place in the fridge for at least 30 minutes to set. Melt the dark chocolate in the microwave or in a small heatproof bowl over a pan of simmering water. Drizzle the bars with melted chocolate and salted caramel sauce, if using, leave to firm up for 5–10 minutes, then cut into 16 bars. The bars will keep well, stored in an airtight container, for up to 3 days, but are best eaten on the day they are made.

MAKES 16 BARS

PREP TIME:
5 MINS PLUS COOLING

COOKING TIME: 15 MINS

175g butter, cubed, plus
  extra for greasing
75g soft light brown sugar
100g caster sugar
100g mini marshmallows
1 tsp vanilla extract or
  vanilla bean paste
Pinch of sea salt
200g cornflakes
50g dark chocolate,
  chopped
2 tbsp Salted Caramel
  Sauce (see page 152),
  to serve (optional)

You will also need a
20 x 30cm baking tin.

Giant stroopwafels

I absolutely adore stroopwafels. They are the one biscuit I can't help but be tempted by while queuing for a coffee, and I nearly always succumb to the temptation. I've tried and failed to make delicate stroopwafels as perfect in form as those you can buy, but since you need specialist kit that I can't quite justify cramming into my cupboards, the answer is to super-size it. You can use a regular waffle maker or a Scandinavian waffle iron that creates thin heart-shaped waffles to make this delicious buttery treat, sandwiched with a thick cinnamon caramel sauce.

1. Melt the butter for the waffles in a small saucepan over a medium heat or in the microwave and stir in the vanilla. Remove from the heat and beat in the milk, followed by the egg.

2. Combine the flour, baking powder and caster sugar in a large bowl and make a well in the centre. Slowly pour the wet ingredients into the dry, whisking all the time to form a smooth batter. Set your waffle batter aside to rest while you make the cinnamon caramel filling.

3. To make the cinnamon caramel filling, place the sugar and butter in a saucepan over a low heat, stirring occasionally, until the butter has melted and the sugar has dissolved. Stir in the cinnamon and syrup, then continue to cook the caramel for a few minutes until it has come together and is thick and glossy. Remove from the heat.

4. Preheat your waffle maker and cook the waffles according to the machine's instructions. Most machines will take around 2–3 minutes to cook a waffle. You should get 4–6 waffles in total.

5. Sandwich 2 waffles together with cinnamon caramel sauce and serve warm.

MAKES 2–3 GIANT STROOPWAFELS

PREP TIME: 20 MINS

COOKING TIME: 2–3 MINS PER WAFFLE

WAFFLES
100g butter
1 tsp vanilla bean paste or vanilla extract
250ml whole milk
1 egg
175g plain flour
1 tsp baking powder
2 tbsp caster sugar

CINNAMON CARAMEL FILLING
150g soft dark brown sugar
75g butter
1 tsp ground cinnamon
2 tbsp golden syrup

You will also need a waffle maker.

Caramel madeleines with buttered rum sauce

I love having madeleine batter in the fridge because these little cakes bake so quickly that they are perfect for a spontaneous snack. Spiking caramel sauce with dark rum is a cheeky dunking bonus.

1. Melt the butter in a small saucepan over a medium heat until melted and starting to foam and smell nutty. Remove from the heat. Some of the butter solids should have turned brown. Stir in the vanilla and allow to cool briefly.

2. Whisk the brown sugar and eggs in a bowl for 6–7 minutes, using a stand mixer or electric hand-held whisk on high speed, until the mixture is light and thick. You know that enough air is incorporated when you can take the whisk out and the mixture leaves a trail that takes 3 seconds to disappear.

3. Combine the flour and baking powder in a small bowl, then sift it over the egg mixture. Use a metal spoon or a flexible spatula to fold the dry ingredients into the wet ingredients until all the flour is mixed in.

4. Add the butter mixture to the batter, stirring to combine. Cover the bowl with cling film and chill for at least 30 minutes – preferably overnight.

5. Grease the madeleine tin liberally with butter (I use my fingers to make sure all the crevices are coated), lightly dust with flour and place in the freezer to chill. Preheat the oven to 200°C/180°C fan/gas 6.

6. Place 1 heaped teaspoon of batter into each shell. The mixture will spread out as it bakes, so it doesn't need to fill the mould. Bake for 8–10 minutes, until the middle has risen into the classic hump, and they are springy to the touch. Remove from the oven and leave to cool on a wire rack.

7. To make the rum caramel sauce, place the sugar and 4 tablespoons of water in a small saucepan and stir briefly to combine. Set over a medium heat and allow the mixture to bubble for 5–6 minutes until it turns golden brown. Try not to stir the mixture while it caramelises or the sugar might crystallise, but do swirl the pan occasionally if the caramel is colouring unevenly.

8. When the sugar turns dark amber and starts to smell caramelised, remove from the heat and stir in the butter. It will splutter and bubble, so beware.

9. Slowly pour in the double cream and rum, stirring as you add them. Return the mixture to the heat for 1 minute, then stir in the sea salt. Pour the sauce into a heatproof bowl and serve alongside the madeleines as a dip.

MAKES 24 MADELEINES

PREP TIME: 20 MINS PLUS CHILLING

COOKING TIME: 8–10 MINS

MADELEINES
100g butter, plus extra for greasing
1 tsp vanilla bean paste
100g soft light brown sugar
2 eggs
100g plain flour, plus extra for dusting
½ tsp baking powder

RUM CARAMEL SAUCE
125g caster sugar
50g butter
50ml double cream
2 tbsp dark rum
Pinch of flaked sea salt

You will also need a madeleine tray.

Brown butter caramel tartlets

These tarts are decadent, with a fudgy toffee-like centre and chewy oat base. Butter is one of my favourite ingredients. It's so versatile, and it's the backbone of a lot of bakes but the star in these tartlets. Browning butter is a simple process that creates a delicate nuttiness and unusual flavour that deserves its moment in the spotlight.

1. Preheat the oven to 180°C/160°C fan/gas 4 and place the tartlet tins on a baking tray.

2. Blitz the Hobnobs in a food processor until they form fine crumbs. Alternatively, place them in a large plastic bag, seal and bash them with a rolling pin. Transfer the crushed biscuits to a bowl and stir in the brown sugar.

3. Place all the butter (for both the crust and the filling) in a small saucepan and heat until completely melted. Continue to cook the butter over a medium heat for a few minutes until it starts to foam and smell nutty, then remove from the heat. Some of the solids in the butter will have turned brown. Add 2 tablespoons of the browned butter to the crushed biscuits and stir to combine. The mixture should clump together – add a little more melted butter if it doesn't.

4. Press the biscuit crust mixture firmly into the tartlet tins, creating an even layer on the bottom and sides of each tart, then chill in the fridge while you make the filling.

5. Stir the caster sugar, soft brown sugar and remaining browned butter together in a bowl with a wooden spoon until well combined. Pour in the double cream and beat for a few minutes, then stir in the egg yolks and beat again. The filling mixture should be smooth and glossy.

6. Remove the tartlet cases from the fridge and divide the filling evenly among them. Bake the tarts for 15–20 minutes until the caramel is puffy and set round the edges but still wobbly in the centre. Allow to cool for 10 minutes in the tin, then remove and enjoy warm or, better still, chill for a few hours for fudgy, chewy tarts.

MAKES 8 MINI TARTLETS

PREP TIME: 20 MINS
PLUS COOLING

COOKING TIME:
15–20 MINS

CRUST
200g Hobnobs or other
    oat-based biscuits
1 tbsp soft light brown
    sugar
50g butter

FILLING
100g butter
150g caster sugar
100g soft light brown
    sugar
100ml double cream
4 egg yolks

You will also need 4 x 8cm fluted tartlet tins.

Malted millionaire's slices

These delicious slices have a biscuit base instead of the traditional shortbread, so they are much quicker to whip up. Malted biscuits have a very nostalgic feel about them, and these layered treats embrace that childish spirit with gooey malted caramel, marbled chocolate and crushed Maltesers. You can find malt extract in health-food shops or online.

1. Grease the tin and line it with baking parchment. To make the base, blitz the biscuits with the Maltesers in a food processor until they resemble fine breadcrumbs. Alternatively, place the biscuits and Maltesers in a plastic bag, seal the bag and bash them with a rolling pin. Transfer the crumbs to a bowl.

2. Melt the butter in a saucepan or in the microwave, then pour it into the crumbs and stir so the ingredients are really well combined. Tip the buttered crumbs into the prepared tin and use a spatula to firmly press them down into an even layer. Pop the tin into the fridge or freezer to chill while you make the caramel.

3. Place the light brown sugar, butter, condensed milk, golden syrup and malt extract (if using) in a large saucepan and heat gently, stirring until the butter has melted. Turn the heat up and allow to simmer for 10–12 minutes, stirring all the time, until the mixture is thick and has a golden caramel colour.

4. Pour the hot caramel filling over the chilled base, leave it to cool for a couple of minutes and return it to the fridge or freezer for 10–15 minutes until it sets firm.

5. When the caramel has set, melt the dark chocolate in a heatproof bowl set over a pan of simmering water or in the microwave. Melt the white chocolate in the same way and spoon it into a piping bag (if you wish). Pour the dark chocolate over the set base, then drizzle over the white chocolate and run a skewer or cocktail stick across the top to marble the chocolate. Press in the halved Maltesers and leave to set, then remove from the tin and cut into 24 slices. The millionaire's slices will keep, stored in an airtight container, for up to 1 week.

MAKES 24 SLICES

PREP TIME: 25 MINS
PLUS CHILLING

COOKING TIME:
10–12 MINS

BASE
250g malted milk biscuits
    or digestive biscuits
50g Maltesers
100g butter, plus extra
    for greasing

CARAMEL
100g soft light brown
    sugar
100g butter
1 x 397g tin condensed
    milk
50g golden syrup
1 tbsp malt extract
    (optional)

TOPPING
200g dark chocolate,
    chopped
50g white chocolate,
    chopped
25g Maltesers, halved

You will also need a
20 x 30cm baking tin
and a disposable piping
bag (if using).

Butterscotch thumbprint cookies

Butterscotch is a richer version of caramel, made with molasses-rich brown sugar instead of caster sugar. You can use light or dark brown sugar, depending how intense you want the treacle flavour to be. These are ideal biscuits for kids to make because they are so straightforward, and it is good fun digging your thumb into the centre of each biscuit to make room for the butterscotch. Jam or a citrus curd can also be used to fill the centres.

1. Place the flour, sugar and cold butter in a large mixing bowl and rub the butter into the flour with your fingertips until the mixture resembles fine breadcrumbs. Add the milk and mix until the cookie dough clumps together, then get your hands in and knead the dough lightly until it forms a ball. Wrap in cling film and chill for around 30 minutes.

2. Preheat the oven to 200°C/180°C fan/gas 6 and line a baking sheet with baking parchment. Melt the butter for the butterscotch filling in a saucepan, then stir in the sugar and cream. Bring the mixture to a gentle simmer and allow to bubble for 4–5 minutes, stirring occasionally to stop the butterscotch sticking to the bottom of the pan and burning. Remove the butterscotch from the heat and stir in the vanilla and sea salt to taste, then pour into a clean jar or small bowl until ready to use.

3. Remove the dough from the fridge, unwrap it and use a teaspoon to scoop small amounts of mixture and roll them into balls (about 20 balls in total). Arrange the balls on the lined baking sheet, leaving a small space around each to allow for spreading. Push gently into the centre of each ball with your thumb to make a small cavity. Put ½ teaspoon of butterscotch into the centre of each cookie and bake for 12–14 minutes or until golden round the edges.

4. Remove from the oven and leave to harden on the baking sheet, being careful not to touch the centre of the cookies because they will be very hot!

MAKES ABOUT 20 BISCUITS

PREP TIME: 15 MINS PLUS CHILLING

COOKING TIME: 12–14 MINS

COOKIE DOUGH
175g plain flour
75g caster sugar
100g cold butter, diced
1 tbsp milk

BUTTERSCOTCH CENTRE
50g butter
100g soft dark or light brown sugar
100ml double cream
1 tbsp vanilla extract or vanilla bean paste
Pinch of flaked sea salt, or to taste

CARAMEL

Treacle tart

It always feels wrong that a traditional treacle tart doesn't include any treacle! My version is sticky with treacle and syrup, giving it a wintry caramel-like flavour. Make your own breadcrumbs by blitzing crustless white bread in a food processor until it forms crumbs.

1. Place the flour in a large bowl and add the butter. Rub the cubes into the flour using your fingertips until the mixture resembles fine breadcrumbs. Gradually add 4 tablespoons of cold water, a little at a time (you might not need it all), stirring it into the butter and flour with a round-ended knife until it clumps together to form a dough. Shape the dough into a ball, wrap it in cling film and place in the fridge for 30 minutes or until you are ready to use it.

2. Preheat the oven to 180°C/160°C fan/gas 4 and lightly grease the tart tin with butter. Unwrap the chilled dough and roll it out on a lightly floured worktop to roughly the thickness of a £1 coin, then press it into the tin using floured fingers. Prick the base with a fork to stop the pastry rising, then line the pastry case with baking parchment and fill with baking beans, or dry rice or lentils, if you don't have baking beans. Bake the pastry for 15 minutes, then remove the parchment and filling, and bake for a further 5 minutes until golden brown.

3. While the pastry is baking, make the filling. Place the golden syrup, black treacle and butter in a saucepan over a medium heat and stir until the butter has melted. Remove from the heat and stir in the lemon juice and milk, then allow to cool briefly before beating in the egg.

4. Fill the baked pastry case with the breadcrumbs, then pour over the syrup mixture. Make sure all the breadcrumbs are coated and smooth the top with a spatula. Bake for 25–30 minutes until golden brown and bubbling. Remove from the oven and serve the tart hot or cold with crème fraîche and a little lemon zest to offset the sweetness.

SERVES 12

PREP TIME: 25 MINS
PLUS CHILLING

COOKING TIME:
25–30 MINS

PASTRY
250g plain flour, plus
  extra for dusting
125g cold butter, diced,
  plus extra for greasing

FILLING
400g golden syrup
50g black treacle
50g butter
Juice of ½ lemon
2 tbsp milk
1 egg, beaten
100g fresh breadcrumbs
Crème fraîche and grated
  lemon zest, to serve

You will also need a
23cm-round loose-
bottomed tart tin.

Burnt caramel banana bread

I'm fully aware that 'burnt' doesn't sound like something you'd do to a bake intentionally. Sometimes the bitter notes from slightly burnt sugar work perfectly to offset sweetness. This is the case in banana bread, with the dark caramel balancing the sweet banana as well as creating an almost bejewelled appearance.

1. Preheat the oven to 170°C/150°C fan/gas 3. Grease the loaf tin with butter and line it with baking parchment. Line a baking tray with baking parchment.

2. Place the sugar in a small heavy-based saucepan or frying pan and place over a medium heat. Leave the sugar to melt without stirring. After a few minutes, the edges will have started to liquefy. Swirl the pan to re-distribute the caramelised sugar over the base of the pan, which will encourage the remaining dry sugar to melt.

3. When the caramel is a dark amber colour and just on the verge of being burnt (this should take 4–5 minutes), remove the pan from the heat and pour the caramel into the lined baking tray to cool completely.

4. Using the same pan, slice 2 of the bananas into thin discs and sauté them over a medium–high heat with 25g of the butter and all the brown sugar for 4–5 minutes until the bananas are starting to soften. Remove from the heat and mash with a fork or potato masher until the mixture is mostly smooth with just a few lumps of banana – the slices should disintegrate fairly quickly. Stir the remaining butter into the warm mashed banana and allow it to melt.

5. Combine the flour and baking powder in a large bowl. Pour the milk into the mashed banana mixture and stir to combine, followed by the eggs. Pour the wet ingredients into the dry ingredients and beat until the mixture is smooth and no lumps of flour remain. Don't over-beat the mixture at this stage or the resulting banana bread will be tough. Scrape the batter into the prepared tin and smooth the top.

6. Break up the cooled caramel into shards and smash it to a chunky powder, either in a food processor or in a plastic bag with a rolling pin. Spoon the powdered caramel over the top of the cake mixture, spreading it out into an even layer. Split the remaining banana in half lengthways and press it into the mixture, cut-sides up.

7. Bake the cake for 45–50 minutes or until the cake is risen and golden and a skewer inserted into the centre comes out clean. The caramel on top should have melted and formed a dark crust. Remove from the oven and cool for 5 minutes in the tin, then transfer to a wire rack to cool completely.

MAKES 1 LOAF

PREP TIME: 25 MINS

COOKING TIME: 45–50 MINS

75g caster sugar
3 ripe bananas, peeled
100g butter, plus extra for greasing
125g soft light brown sugar
275g plain flour
1 tsp baking powder
125ml milk
2 eggs, beaten

You will also need a 23 x 12cm (1 litre) loaf tin.

Coffee caramel monkey bread

While I have no idea why this bread is called monkey bread, one thing I do know is that it is absolutely delicious! Be sure to eat this fresh from the oven while it's still warm, as the caramel will be molten and the pieces of dough will pull apart perfectly.

1. Heat the milk in a small saucepan with the butter over a low heat until the cubes of butter are completely melted, then remove from the heat and set to one side to allow the mixture to cool for a few minutes.

2. Place the flour in a large bowl and add the yeast to one side of the bowl and the salt and sugar to the other. If you put the salt directly on the yeast it may kill it, which will stop your dough from rising.

3. Beat the eggs into the lukewarm milk mixture (it should feel just slightly warm when you stick a finger into it). Gradually add this to the dry mixture, stirring all the time, until a sticky dough forms. You may not need to add all the milk mixture – you want to add just enough to make a sticky but not wet dough.

4. Tip the dough on to a lightly oiled worktop and knead it for 10–15 minutes or until it is no longer sticky and has become smooth and elastic. Place the dough into an oiled bowl, cover with cling film and leave in a warm place for 1–2 hours or until doubled in size.

5. Grease the bundt tin with butter. Melt the butter for the coffee caramel coating in a small saucepan and combine the brown sugar with the coffee powder in a small bowl. Remove the pan of melted butter from the heat. Tip the dough on to a floured worktop and divide and roll into 50 small dough balls, each one similar in diameter to a 2p coin (2.5cm).

6. Roll each dough ball in the melted butter, then in the coffee-sugar mixture until thoroughly coated. Randomly scatter the dough balls into the bundt tin, trying not to squash them down. They will touch and stick together as the dough proves. Tip any remaining butter or coffee-sugar mixture over the top of the dough, then cover the tin with cling film and leave the dough to rise for 1 hour.

7. Preheat the oven to 180°C/160°C fan/gas 4. Bake the monkey bread for 30–35 minutes until well risen and golden. The sugar should have caramelised and be bubbling up. Remove from the oven and allow the bread to cool for 5 minutes in the tin, then invert on to a plate and tap sharply before lifting up the tin to remove the bread in one piece. Don't let the bread get too cool in the tin or the caramel will harden, and it will be impossible to remove. Serve the bread as a delicious centrepiece dessert or indulgent breakfast!

MAKES 1 LOAF

PREP TIME:
25 MINS PLUS 2–3 HOURS PROVING

COOKING TIME:
30–35 MINS

200ml milk
75g unsalted butter, cubed, plus extra for greasing the tin
500g strong plain flour, plus extra for dusting
1 x 7g sachet fast-action dried yeast
1 tsp fine salt
50g caster sugar
2 eggs
Oil, for greasing

COFFEE CARAMEL COATING
100g butter
200g soft light brown sugar
1 tbsp instant espresso powder

You will also need a large bundt tin.

Sticky toffee pudding cake

Sticky toffee pudding is a longstanding favourite of the British population, so a glorious cake showcasing the best elements of the pudding is sure to be a crowd-pleaser. Let the thick toffee sauce drip down the sides of the cake – it's a proper messy pudding!

1. Preheat the oven to 180°C/160°C fan/gas 4. Grease the cake tins and line them with baking parchment.

2. Heat the butter, sugar, treacle and golden syrup together in a large saucepan, stirring until the butter has melted and the sugar has dissolved. Remove the pan from the heat.

3. Gradually pour the milk into the saucepan with the hot mixture, whisking continuously, then beat in the eggs until well combined. Sift the flour and bicarbonate of soda together into the saucepan and whisk until smooth. Fold through the chopped dates.

4. Divide the mixture evenly among the prepared tins, either by counting equal spoonfuls of mixture or by weighing the tins, then bake the 3 cakes for 30–35 minutes or until firm and a skewer inserted into the centre comes out clean. Remove from the oven and leave to cool briefly in the tins then transfer to a wire rack to cool completely.

5. While the cakes are cooling, make the toffee sauce. Place the double cream, treacle, sugar and butter in a saucepan and heat gently until the grains of sugar have dissolved. Turn up the heat and allow to boil for 5 minutes or until the sauce thickly coats the back of a metal spoon. Pour into a heatproof and microwave-safe jug, and set aside to cool.

6. To make the buttercream, briefly beat the butter in a large bowl or the bowl of a stand mixer to soften it, then add the icing sugar a little at a time, making sure each addition of sugar is well incorporated into the mix before adding more. Beat for 5–10 minutes until really light and fluffy, then add 100ml of the cooled toffee sauce and beat for a few more minutes.

7. To assemble the cake, place the first layer on a cake stand or serving plate on a turntable, if you have one. Use a small amount of the buttercream to secure the base layer to the plate or stand and top with about one-fifth of the buttercream. Use a palette knife to spread the buttercream right to the edges of the cake then top with the second layer of sponge. Repeat the buttercream process and place the final layer on top.

SERVES 12

PREP TIME: 1–1¼ HOURS

COOKING TIME: 30–35 MINS

STICKY TOFFEE SPONGE
200g butter, plus extra for greasing
250g dark muscovado sugar
100g black treacle
100g golden syrup
200ml milk
2 eggs
250g plain flour
1 tsp bicarbonate of soda
200g chopped dates, preferably Medjool

TOFFEE SAUCE
250ml double cream
1 tbsp black treacle
150g demerara sugar
100g butter

BUTTERCREAM
200g unsalted butter, softened
300g icing sugar
100ml toffee sauce (see above)

TO DECORATE
100g pecan nuts, chopped into small pieces
4 Medjool dates, stoned

CARAMEL

8. Cover the top and sides of the cake with the remaining buttercream, scraping the excess away from the sides with a large palette knife so that the cake is thinly and evenly coated and the layers show through. The top should be smooth and the edges neat. Place the cake in the fridge for at least 30 minutes for the buttercream to set.

9. Gently heat the remaining caramel sauce in the microwave or a small pan over a low heat, until it is just pourable but not warm enough to melt the buttercream. Pour the sauce directly over the centre of the cake and push it right to the edges, gently teasing it down the edges to create drips. Sprinkle the pecan nuts around the edge of half the cake, then slice the Medjool dates into rounds and decorate the top with them.

You will also need 3 x 18cm-round cake tins, a cake stand or large plate and a turntable.

Cheese

Understanding *Cheese*

Of all the ingredients in this book, this is the one I crave most and was most excited to write about. Cheese is salty and satisfying at any time of day, from cream cheese bagels to naughty midnight nibbles. If it's a Dairylea triangle or a cave-aged Cheddar that gets your mouth watering, expect no judgement here.

Cheese-glorifying meals rank among the best. Macaroni cheese is my guilty pleasure. A cheese fondue or a raclette are top winter meals. When else is it deemed appropriate to douse all foods in oozing melted cheese? I throw in all kinds of cheese and dip in anything from French bread to chorizo.

My first job was working on the cheese counter at a supermarket as a Saturday girl. I had to hide my enthusiasm from my less-excited colleagues and act as normally as possible while in charge of more varieties of cheese than I had ever seen. It took all my self-control to stop myself from eating the crumbs that fell off cheese blocks as I was slicing them for customers. I revelled in the opportunity to learn about the origins and flavour profiles of the different cheeses and would stand behind the counter dreaming up the dishes I could create.

The number of different types of cheese available to us today is astounding. The source of milk (sheep, goat, cow or buffalo), the method of production (brined, washed rind, stretched) and the length and conditions of maturation (months, years, in caves or barrels) all change the nature of the final product. We can choose from cheeses injected with mould, stinky cheeses washed in wine and mild cheeses that can be made at home, like ricotta or mascarpone. All have their own special uses in baking, whether that be melted into a bread or whipped into a cheesecake.

Meltability

Cheese has this much-adored affinity to melt into gooey, stretchy puddles. High-moisture soft cheeses (such as brie, mozzarella and cream cheese) are better for melting than hard cheeses as the high water content allows the cheese to liquefy with ease when heated. Hard cheeses with a low moisture content, such as Parmesan, won't completely liquefy – they generally hold their shape, making them ideal for making crisps or adding texture to bakes. *See:* Parmesan and Chipotle Crisps

Maturity

Months or years of maturation can transform a fresh, creamy cheese into a hard cheese with a sharp, intense flavour. Maturation can also have the opposite effect on texture, with soft cheeses such as Brie or Camembert becoming softer. You can use both in baking, but aged hard cheeses melt more reluctantly. *See:* Triple Cheese Gougères

Acid or rennet?

Cheese is made by separating milk into curds and whey, then processing the curds. Acid or the enzyme rennet are added to milk to start the separation, and the resulting cheese from each responds to heat in different ways. Heating a rennet-set cheese such as Camembert or Cheddar generally results in the proteins in the cheese breaking down and melting, which makes them perfect for dipping or using to bind other ingredients. The proteins in acid-set cheeses, such as paneer or ricotta, hold together more tightly the longer they are heated, so they don't melt, making them great for fillings or grilling. *See:* Baked Époisses with Prosciutto Dippers

Smoked cheese

Cheese smoked over wood chips adds a wonderful smokiness to bakes and often has a much stronger flavour than its unsmoked counterpart, so you can use a slightly smaller quantity. Authentic smoked cheeses should have a golden-brown rind or orange speckles; avoid artificially flavoured smoked cheeses, as the flavour is compromised by the chemical process they go through. *See:* Smoked Cheddar Welsh Rarebit

Baked Époisses fondue with prosciutto dippers

When properly ripe, Époisses is so soft it is almost liquid at room temperature. This makes it perfect for a quick hot bite as you just need to warm it through and you've got an instant fondue! You could use Camembert or Brie as a substitute, but I adore the tangy saltiness that Époisses has in abundance. It's rich and indulgent (and very pungent!), but hits the spot when you need a cheese hit.

1. Preheat the oven to 220°C/200°C fan/gas 7. Finely chop the garlic and rosemary with a knife or crush them in a pestle and mortar. Combine the garlic and rosemary with the oil in a bowl and massage it over the skin of the cheese.

2. Place the cheese in its box in a small ovenproof dish and bake it for 10 minutes or until it is bubbling and molten inside.

3. Slice each piece of bread into 4 strips and wrap each with a slice of prosciutto. Arrange the breadsticks on a baking tray and place in the oven above the cheese. Bake for 5–10 minutes until the bread is toasted and the ham is crisp.

4. Cut a hole in the hot baked cheese. The centre should be molten and gooey. Serve immediately with the breadsticks and crudités to dip – I like strips of red pepper and asparagus tips best.

SERVES 2 AS A SNACK

PREP TIME: 5 MINS

COOKING TIME: 5–10 MINS

1 garlic clove
Needles from 1 sprig of rosemary
1 tsp olive oil
1 x 250g ripe Époisses cheese
2 slices of crusty bread
8 slices of prosciutto ham
Selection of crudités, to serve

Parmesan and chipotle crisps

You don't get a simpler snack than these cheese crisps. Proper Parmesan has a strong, punchy flavour as it is allowed to mature for at least 12 months, and the spicy smokiness from the chipotle complements it perfectly. I love the lacy appearance of the melted cheese, not dissimilar to a savoury Florentine. You can use any hard cheese: Gouda or aged Comté work very well. Make sure that it is good quality and cut from a block of cheese for the best taste – powdery shakers of pre-grated Parmesan won't work here!

MAKES ABOUT 30 CRISPS

PREP TIME: 5 MINS

COOKING TIME: 5–7 MINS

100g Parmesan (Parmigiano-Reggiano is best)
1 small dried chipotle chilli or ½ tsp chipotle powder
Freshly ground black pepper, to season

1. Preheat the oven to 200°C/180°C fan/gas 6 and line a large baking sheet with baking parchment.

2. Finely grate the Parmesan into a small bowl and crush the chipotle chilli in a pestle and mortar until it is finely ground (if using a whole dried chilli). Add the ground chipotle or chipotle powder to the grated cheese and season with black pepper. Mix the ingredients together until they are well combined.

3. Arrange the cheese mixture into small rounds on the baking sheet, making sure they are all a similar size and an even thickness. I use a small round cookie cutter (about 3cm diameter) as a guide. If they are too heaped, the centres will be chewy, and they won't become crisp.

4. Bake the crisps for 5–7 minutes or until melted and just starting to colour. Remove from the oven and allow to cool for a few minutes on the baking sheet, or until firm enough to pick up, then tip carefully into a bowl and enjoy.

Smoked Cheddar Welsh rarebit

Cheese on toast is my weakness and ultimate comfort food. This is what I treat myself to after a busy day out in the cold or enjoy as a secret midnight snack. There is nothing wrong with plain and simple cheese on toast, but I often find that the cheese separates and instead of the oozing snack that I crave, I'm left with oily split cheese on dampened bread. Rarebit solves this problem. Putting a little more effort into a silky smooth cheese sauce that bubbles up into a gooey blanket over the nutty brown toast is well worth it. If you're making this for children or don't fancy cracking open a can of beer, use milk instead of beer to make the topping.

1. Melt the butter in a small saucepan then stir in the flour to make a paste. Cook the paste for a minute or so – this allows the starch in the flour to cook out, which results in a smoother sauce. Gradually pour in the beer (or milk), stirring all the time to prevent any lumps from forming.

2. Whisk in the mustard and Worcestershire sauce, then add the grated cheese to the pan and heat until the cheese has just melted. Taste the sauce and add more mustard or Worcestershire sauce, if you wish. Remove the pan from the heat and set to one side while you prepare the bread.

3. Preheat the grill to medium–high, and toast and butter the bread on both sides. Beat the egg yolk into the cheese mixture until smooth, then spread the rarebit mixture evenly on the toast, making sure it goes right to the edges. Grill for a few minutes until browned and bubbling, then serve immediately.

SERVES 2

PREP TIME: 10 MINS

**COOKING TIME:
5 MINS**

25g butter
25g plain flour
75ml beer or milk
1 tsp Dijon mustard
1 tsp Worcestershire
    sauce
125g smoked Cheddar or
    other smoked cheese,
    grated
2 slices of crusty
    wholemeal bread or
    sourdough
Butter, for spreading
1 egg yolk

Tartiflette potato skins

Tartiflette is a French alpine snack of buttery potato with bacon and onions, all smothered in melted cheese. It is designed to be served up by the plateful to exhausted skiers or snowboarders to boost energy levels, but that doesn't stop me wolfing it down in mini-potato-skin form on a lazy Saturday afternoon after doing no exercise whatsoever. Try to find reblochon cheese to make this luxurious dish as authentic as possible, but Port Salut or even Camembert are good substitutes.

SERVES 2–3
PREP TIME: 20 MINS
COOKING TIME: 25–30 MINS

7–8 small waxy potatoes
1 tbsp olive oil
1 tbsp butter
1 small onion or shallot, finely chopped
100g smoked bacon lardons
100ml double cream
200g reblochon cheese
Freshly ground black pepper, to season
Snipped chives and crème fraîche, to serve

1. Preheat the oven to 200°C/180°C fan/gas 6. Cut the potatoes in half lengthways and run a sharp knife around the edges of each half, cutting into the potato but being careful not to cut all the way through. Leave about 5mm of potato on the skin so the case is strong enough to hold a filling. Use a dessertspoon to scoop out the middle of the potato and set the centres to one side. Drizzle the potato skins with the olive oil and bake on a baking tray for 15 minutes.

2. Slice the potato that has been scooped out into roughly 5mm cubes. Melt half the butter in a frying pan over a medium heat and add the onion and bacon. Sauté until the onions have softened and the bacon starts to become crisp, then tip the cooked onion and bacon into a small bowl.

3. Melt the remaining butter in the frying pan and fry the potato cubes for 5–10 minutes until browned on the outside and cooked through. Tip the onion and bacon mixture back into the pan and add the double cream, season with black pepper and stir to combine. Remove from the heat, slice half the reblochon into small cubes and fold the cubes into the mixture.

4. Spoon the filling into the baked-potato-skin cavities. Finely slice the remaining reblochon into long thin strips and lay the strips over the top of the filling, then bake the skins for 10–15 minutes or until bubbling and golden. Remove from the oven and serve with crème fraîche and snipped chives.

Triple cheese gougères

Why have one cheese when you can have three? These choux pastry puffs have a complex flavour created by combining different cheeses; I use a mix of sweet Comté, tangy Gouda and umami-rich Parmesan. They make perfect canapés, but be warned that if you decide to serve these before a meal, your guests will gorge on them before they get near the dining table! Feel free to use any kind of cheese in these gougères – hard cheeses work better than soft.

MAKES 30 GOUGÈRES

PREP TIME: 20 MINS

COOKING TIME: 15–20 MINS

75g butter, diced
1 tsp caster sugar
½ tsp salt
50g plain flour
50g strong bread flour
3 eggs
50g Comté, grated
50g Old Amsterdam Gouda, grated
25g Parmesan, grated
Freshly ground black pepper, to season

1. Preheat the oven to 200°C/180°C fan/gas 6 and line 2 large baking sheets with baking parchment.

2. Place the butter, sugar, salt and 125ml of water in a small saucepan over a medium–high heat. Bring the mixture to a rolling boil and when all the butter has melted, add the flour in one go and vigorously beat the mixture with a wooden spoon until a smooth ball of dough forms.

3. Keep the pan on the heat and stir rapidly for a further minute. This cooks the flour and helps dry out the dough so it absorbs more egg, which in turn helps the pastry expand properly when baked. Tip the dough into a bowl and leave it to cool until it has stopped steaming.

4. Beat the eggs together briefly in a small jug. Add the eggs to the cooled dough in 3 separate additions, beating well between each one with a wooden spoon or spatula. It can be quite difficult to work the eggs in, but keep mixing and the dough will turn into a thick paste. It should fall off the spoon and leave a 'V' shape. Stir in the grated Comté and Gouda, and season with black pepper.

5. Use a teaspoon to spoon small balls of dough on to the baking sheets (about 15 on each), leaving a few centimetres between each one so they have room to puff up. Sprinkle them with Parmesan and bake for 15–20 minutes or until golden brown and puffy, then remove from the oven and serve warm.

Butternut squash and feta empanadas

Empanadas are the Spanish version of our well-loved Cornish pasties. These are filled with a spicy butternut-squash filling, offset with salty, tangy feta cheese. I like these warm with a zesty green salad for lunch, or I make mini ones and serve them as party canapés.

MAKES 10 EMPANADAS
PREP TIME: 30 MINS
**COOKING TIME:
20–25 MINS**

1. Preheat the oven to 200°C/180°C fan/gas 6 and line a baking sheet with baking parchment.

2. To make the pastry, tip the flour into a large bowl and add the butter. Rub the cubes into the flour with your fingertips until the mixture resembles fine breadcrumbs. Add the egg and 2 tablespoons of cold water, then mix using a round-ended knife until the mixture starts to clump together. You may need to add a little more cold water to help the pastry come together. Knead the dough briefly in the bowl until smooth, then shape it into a ball, wrap it in cling film and place in the fridge for at least 20 minutes while you make the filling.

3. Melt the butter for the filling in a large frying pan over a medium heat and fry the onion and garlic together until softened. Add the butternut squash cubes and continue to cook for a further 10 minutes. The butternut squash should be tender if you stick a knife into it. Stir in the cumin and paprika or chilli powder and season with salt and pepper before removing from the heat.

4. Roll out the empanada dough on a lightly floured worktop or between 2 sheets of cling film to a thickness of around 3mm. Use a cutter or cut around a plate to make 10cm circles out of the dough. You should get 10 circles once you've re-rolled the offcuts and cut out more.

5. Stir the crumbled feta and chopped sage leaves through the empanada filling and place a tablespoon of filling in the centre of each circle. Brush the edges of the empanadas with water to help them stick together, then pull up the edges and crimp along the middle using your fingers to seal.

6. Place all the empanadas on the lined baking sheet and brush with beaten egg. Bake for 20–25 minutes or until golden brown all over. Remove from the oven and serve warm or at room temperature.

PASTRY
400g plain flour, plus extra for dusting
200g cold butter, cubed
1 egg, beaten

FILLING
25g butter
1 small red onion, roughly chopped
2 garlic cloves, peeled and crushed
400g peeled butternut squash, cut into small cubes
1 tsp ground cumin
1 tsp hot smoked paprika or chilli powder
100g feta, crumbled
Small bunch of sage leaves, finely chopped
1 egg, beaten
Salt and freshly ground black pepper, to season

Cherry and chocolate cheesecake brownies

The contrast between rich dark-chocolate brownie and creamy cheesecake swirl is very striking and what makes these brownies special. Gooey brownies are the bake I'm asked to make most by my boyfriend, closely followed by cheesecake, so this combination always goes down well. Make sure you steal a little bite while it's still warm, to satisfy your craving, but leave most of the tray to cool completely for the optimum texture.

1. Preheat the oven to 180°C/160°C fan/gas 4; grease the brownie tin and line it with baking parchment.

2. Put the sugars and butter in a large saucepan, place over a medium heat and cook, stirring occasionally, until the butter has melted and the sugar has dissolved. The sugar should lose its grainy appearance and the butter will have completely combined with the sugar instead of being a separated layer (this takes a few minutes). Remove from the heat.

3. Add the chopped dark chocolate to the warm sugar and butter mixture, and stir it in until it is completely melted. Leave to cool to room temperature.

4. While the brownie mixture cools, make the cheesecake mixture. Beat the cream cheese in a small bowl with the sugar and egg until smooth, then stir through the vanilla.

5. When the brownie mixture is cool enough to touch comfortably, beat in the eggs. Add the flour and cocoa powder then stir briefly to combine. Scrape the mixture into the lined brownie tin and spread it out, then dollop spoonfuls of the cheesecake mixture over the top. Use a skewer to swirl the cheesecake through the brownie to create a marbled effect, then scatter over the cherries.

6. Bake for 25–30 minutes or until the cheesecake swirls are just beginning to brown around the edges. Remove from the oven and leave to cool. For the best texture, leave the brownie to cool completely in the tin then chill for a few hours before cutting it into squares.

MAKES 15 BROWNIES
PREP TIME: 20 MINS
COOKING TIME:
25–30 MINS

BROWNIE
150g soft light brown sugar
225g caster sugar
200g butter, plus extra for greasing
150g dark chocolate, chopped
3 eggs
100g plain flour
30g cocoa powder
75g fresh black cherries, pitted (fresh is preferable, but you could use tinned)

CHEESECAKE
200g full-fat cream cheese
50g caster sugar
1 egg
1 tsp vanilla extract or vanilla bean paste

You will also need a 20 x 35cm brownie tin.

Cheese and Marmite sausage rolls

I've been eating cheese and Marmite sandwiches for as long as I can remember. Marmite is my mum's favourite food, so it goes in to a lot of our family meals, and we have many novelty pots lining our cupboards. The salty, rich taste enhances the flavour of the pork and works perfectly with the tang of mature Cheddar cheese.

1. Preheat the oven to 200°C/180°C fan/gas 6 and line a baking sheet with baking parchment.

2. Heat the olive oil in a frying pan over a medium heat, add the onion and garlic, and fry until softened and starting to brown. Tip them into a large bowl.

3. Add the sausagemeat to the bowl with 1 tablespoon of the Marmite and season with black pepper. Marmite is very salty, so you shouldn't need to add any extra salt. Mash everything together using a fork or squeeze together using your hands, then stir in the cheese.

4. Lightly dust a worktop with flour and roll out the pastry into a large rectangle, about 35 x 20cm, then slice it in half lengthways to create 2 long rectangles. Spread the remaining Marmite on one half of each piece of pastry lengthways, leaving a 1cm gap at the edges.

5. Divide the sausagemeat mixture in half and roll each half on a floured worktop to make two long sausage shapes. Make sure they are of an even thickness so the sausage rolls are the same size.

6. Place one of the sausagemeat rolls on a pastry strip, making sure it is directly on the top of the Marmite. Brush the exposed pastry with a little beaten egg, then fold the top half over the sausage and use a fork to crimp the edge closed. Repeat with the second pastry strip and sausage filling, then cut each sausage roll into 5 smaller pieces about 7cm in length.

7. Place the sausage rolls on the lined baking sheet, then brush the tops of the rolls with the remaining beaten egg. Make several diagonal cuts on the top of the pastry, then sprinkle with poppy seeds. Bake for 30–35 minutes or until golden brown and cooked through. Some of the cheese and Marmite might have oozed out, but this adds to their rustic charm. Remove from the oven and eat warm, or leave to cool completely and enjoy as an on-the-go snack.

MAKES 10 ROLLS
PREP TIME: 25 MINS
COOKING TIME:
30–35 MINS

1 tbsp olive oil
1 red onion, finely chopped
2 garlic cloves, finely chopped
500g pork sausagemeat
2 tbsp Marmite
100g mature Cheddar cheese, grated
Flour, for dusting
375g block all-butter puff pastry
1 egg, beaten
1 tbsp poppy seeds
Freshly ground black pepper, to season

Mini pork and Stilton pies

Pork pies are the perfect picnic snack, and adding Stilton to the mix adds an acidic undertone that is great with the smoky, salty pork. Hot-water crust pastry is surprisingly easy to make and very forgiving to work with. You handle it while it's hot and mouldable, and you can easily patch up holes without affecting the quality of the pastry.

MAKES 8 MINI PIES

PREP TIME: 25 MINS PLUS COOLING

COOKING TIME: 40–45 MINS

FILLING
150g smoked streaky bacon, finely chopped
400g pork sausagemeat
Small bunch of fresh thyme, leaves chopped
100g Stilton, crumbled
1 egg, beaten
Salt and freshly ground black pepper, to season

PASTRY
100g lard, plus extra for greasing
10g salt
250g strong plain flour
200g plain flour, plus extra for dusting

You will also need a 12-hole muffin tin, a 11cm-round cutter and a 8cm-round cutter.

1. Preheat the oven to 200°C/180°C fan/gas 6; grease each hole of the muffin tin then line them with a thin strip of baking parchment across the bottom that overhangs at the top. This will make it a lot easier to remove the pies once baked.

2. To make the filling, place the bacon in a large bowl with the sausagemeat. Add the thyme, season with salt and pepper, and mix well. Stir through the crumbled Stilton, making sure you don't break down the chunks too much. Set aside.

3. To make the pastry, place the lard and salt in a saucepan with 250ml of water and heat over a medium heat until the water is boiling and the fat has melted.

4. Mix both flours together in a large bowl. Pour the boiling mixture into the flour and stir until a dough has formed. Turn it out on to a floured worktop and knead for a few minutes until the dough is smooth. You will need to move quickly here, because as the dough cools it becomes more difficult to work with.

5. Take two-thirds of the dough and roll it out to a thickness of around 3mm, then use the larger cutter to cut 8 x 11cm rounds from the dough. Press each circle into a muffin tin hole, using your fingers to make sure it is pressed right in. Fill each pastry case right to the top with the pork and Stilton filling.

6. Roll out the remaining pastry dough and cut 8 x 8cm slightly smaller rounds as lids for the pies. Use a skewer to pierce a hole in the top of each pastry lid, then brush the rim of each pie with some of the remaining egg and crimp the lid on to each one.

7. Brush the tops of the pies with the remaining beaten egg and bake for 40–45 minutes until golden brown. Remove from the oven and allow the pies to cool completely in the tin, then carefully remove the pies and chill in the fridge until ready to eat. They will keep in the fridge for up to 1 week.

Fig and Manchego loaf

I made this loaf for my first *Great British Bake Off* audition, and it served me well. The natural sweetness of jammy figs is gorgeous with the almost nutty flavours found in sheep's cheese. Try to buy a mature cheese, as the nutty caramel flavour is much more prominent.

MAKES 1 LOAF

PREP TIME: 25 MINS PLUS PROVING TIME

COOKING TIME: 30–35 MINS

250g strong wholemeal flour

250g strong plain flour, plus extra for dusting

1 tsp fine salt

1 x 7g sachet fast-action dried yeast

2 tbsp olive oil, plus extra for drizzling and greasing

250ml lukewarm water

150g dried figs, roughly chopped

150g Manchego cheese, chopped into small cubes.

Semolina, to dust (optional)

1. Place both the flours in a large bowl, or the bowl of a stand mixer fitted with the dough-hook attachment, and add the salt to one side of the bowl and the yeast to the other. If you put the salt directly on the yeast it may kill it, which will stop your dough from rising.

2. Add the olive oil and three-quarters of the water to the bowl and mix until a rough dough forms. Continue to add the water, mixing until all the flour has been picked up from the sides of the bowl. You might not need all the water, or you might need a little more, depending on the absorbency of the flour.

3. Dust your worktop with flour, tip the dough on to it and knead by hand for about 10 minutes (or using the stand-mixer dough hook), until the dough is smooth and elastic. Drizzle oil into the bowl you used to mix the dough, then place the dough back in the bowl, cover with cling film and leave to rise at room temperature for 1–3 hours until doubled in size.

4. Tip the risen dough out of the bowl on to a lightly floured worktop and fold it in on itself a few times to knock out any large air bubbles. Roll out the dough into a large rectangle and sprinkle the figs and Manchego over the surface. Roll up tightly, enclosing all the filling ingredients. Rolling the loaf in this way should ensure an even distribution of the filling ingredients.

5. Bring the dough coil back into a ball and shape it by folding the outside edges into the centre to form a ball with a taut surface. Place the dough on a baking sheet dusted with semolina, if using, or lined with baking parchment, cover it with a plastic bag or oiled cling film and leave to rise for at least 1 hour at room temperature. Using semolina stops the dough sticking and gives the bread a great crunch underneath.

6. Preheat the oven to 240°C/220°C fan/gas 8 and place a roasting tin in the bottom of the oven to heat up. When the dough has nearly doubled in size again, score the top using a serrated knife and put it in the centre of the oven. Pour a mugful of water into the empty roasting tin to create steam, which will stop the bread from immediately forming a crust, therefore allowing it to expand more in the oven. Bake the loaf for 30–35 minutes or until the outside is a dark brown colour. The bread should feel hollow when tapped underneath. Allow the loaf to cool on a wire rack.

Gouda and smoked paprika pretzels

The train journey from London to home is painfully slow, and I often find myself waiting at a freezing cold station next to an amazing hot-pretzel vendor. I can never resist one of their freshly baked knots; the ones smothered in cheese are my favourite. The go-to guilty snack makes the long train journey much more bearable! It's easy to make your own pretzels, which, curiously, are boiled before they are baked, much like a bagel. This prevents them from rising too much in the oven, giving them a dense and chewy texture. I use an aged Gouda to give the pretzels a tangy flavour, but any hard cheese will work well.

1. Put the butter in a small saucepan with the milk. Heat over a low heat until the cubes of butter are completely melted, then set to one side to allow the mixture to cool for a few minutes.

2. Place the flour in a large bowl, or the bowl of a stand mixer fitted with the dough-hook attachment, and add the yeast to one side of the bowl and the salt and sugar to the other. If you put the salt directly on the yeast it may kill it, which will stop your dough from rising.

3. Gradually add the milk and butter mixture to the dry mixture, stirring all the time, until a sticky dough forms. You may not need to add all the milk mixture – you want to add just enough to form a sticky but not wet dough.

4. Tip the dough on to a lightly oiled worktop and knead for 10–15 minutes or until it is no longer sticky and has become smooth and elastic. Alternatively, knead using the dough-hook attachment on the stand mixer for 5 minutes. Place the dough in an oiled bowl, cover with cling film and leave in a warm place for 1–2 hours or until doubled in size.

5. When the dough has risen, preheat the oven to 210°C/190°C fan/gas 6 and line 2 large baking sheets with baking parchment. Tip the risen dough out of the bowl on to an oiled worktop and fold it in on itself a couple of times to knock out any large air bubbles.

...CONTINUED

MAKES 12 PRETZELS

PREP TIME: 45 MINS PLUS PROVING

COOKING TIME: 20–25 MINS

75g unsalted butter, cubed
200ml whole milk
500g strong plain flour
1 x 7g sachet fast-action dried yeast
1 tsp fine salt
2 tbsp caster sugar
Oil, for greasing
3 tbsp bicarbonate of soda
1 egg, beaten
100g aged Gouda, grated
2 tsp hot smoked paprika

Gouda and smoked paprika pretzels

6. Divide the dough into 12 pieces. To shape the pretzels, take a piece of dough and roll it into a long rope shape that is slightly thinner at the ends. Take both ends of the rope and twist them together once, then lay the ends down over the bottom loop and press in to create a classic pretzel shape. Place on a baking sheet and cover with a tea towel to stop the dough drying out while you shape the remaining dough.

7. Bring 1.5 litres of water to the boil in a saucepan. When the water is boiling, add the bicarbonate of soda and stir in until it stops fizzing. Turn the heat down and leave the mixture at a low simmer.

8. Carefully lower the pretzels into the saucepan, a few at a time, and poach for around 30 seconds each, flipping the pretzels halfway through. Remove from the water and dry the bottoms on a piece of kitchen paper before placing on a baking sheet. Brush the pretzels with beaten egg and sprinkle with the grated cheese and smoked paprika, then bake for 20–25 minutes until the cheese has melted and the pretzels are golden brown all over.

9. Remove from the oven and allow the pretzels to cool for 5 minutes on the baking sheets, then enjoy warm. These are best eaten on the day they are made but can be refreshed by warming up in the oven for the next few days.

Stuffed bagelballs

If you ever find yourself in New York, it would be rude not to seek out a famous New York bagel at least once. I stumbled across something even better while sitting in a café in the city – bagelballs. These were one of the best things I ate there and that's a big accolade, considering how spoilt for choice you are in the Big Apple. Bagelballs have all the chewy, dense deliciousness of a bagel but instead of a hollow middle, the centre holds a cream-cheese surprise. Biting into the rich, creamy centre is a delicious contrast to the chewy, seeded exterior. I tried all different kinds, with sweet and savoury fillings, but my favourite was the herby cream-cheese centre so that is what I've recreated here.

1. Place the flour in a large bowl, or the bowl of a stand mixer fitted with the dough-hook attachment, and add the yeast to one side and the salt to the other. If you put the salt directly on the yeast it may kill it, which will stop your dough from rising.

2. Add 1 tablespoon of the honey or malt extract and three-quarters of the water, and mix with a spoon or with the dough-hook attachment on the mixer. Add the rest of the water gradually, mixing until a soft dough forms. You might not need all the water, or you might need a little more, depending on the absorbency of the flour.

3. Knead the dough for 5–10 minutes on a lightly floured worktop (or for 5 minutes in a stand mixer) until it is smooth and elastic, then place in an oiled bowl, cover with a damp tea towel or sheet of oiled cling film and leave to rise at room temperature for 1–3 hours until doubled in size.

4. While the dough is rising, beat the cream cheese for the filling with the basil until smooth. Season to taste with salt and pepper. Line a baking sheet with baking parchment or cling film, then spoon or pipe 24 small balls of the cream cheese mixture on to the sheet. Freeze the cream cheese balls for at least 30 minutes until solidified.

5. Preheat the oven to 200°C/180°C fan/gas 6 and line a large baking sheet with baking parchment. Half-fill a large saucepan with water and bring it to the boil, then stir in the bicarbonate of soda and remaining honey or malt extract and reduce the heat to a gentle simmer.

MAKES 24 BAGELBALLS

PREP TIME: 45 MINS PLUS PROVING

COOKING TIME: 15–20 MINS

BAGELBALLS
500g strong plain flour, plus extra for dusting
1 x 7g sachet fast-action dried yeast
1 tsp fine salt
2 tbsp honey or malt extract
250ml lukewarm water
1 tbsp bicarbonate of soda
1 egg, beaten
Poppy seeds and sesame seeds, to sprinkle

FILLING
200g full-fat cream cheese
Small bunch of fresh basil leaves, finely chopped
Freshly ground black pepper and sea salt, to season

6. Tip the risen dough out of the bowl on to a lightly floured worktop, knock it back and briefly knead it to get rid of any large air bubbles, then divide it into 24 even-sized pieces. Roll each piece into a dough ball then remove the cream cheese from the freezer.

7. Take one of the balls of dough and use a rolling pin to flatten it slightly (you don't want it too thin or the cheese will burst out) then place a ball of cream cheese in the centre. Fold the dough up around the cream cheese, pinching at the top to completely seal it inside. It's important that the centre is tightly enclosed, and the dough completely sealed, or the filling will burst and leak out in the water or in the oven. Place the rolled ball seam-side down on the baking sheet and repeat with the other pieces of dough.

8. Gently drop the balls into the simmering water and boil them, a few at a time, for 1 minute. They will sink when you drop them in but should rise to the top as they cook. Remove with a slotted spoon and place back on the baking sheet seam-side down.

9. Brush the boiled bagelballs with egg using a pastry brush and sprinkle over the seeds. Bake for 15–20 minutes or until dark golden brown. Some of the balls might explode but will still taste just as good! Remove from the oven and allow to cool briefly on the baking sheet before eating warm or cold as a snack.

Alcohol

Understanding *Alcohol*

It seems almost humorous to write a chapter on how to satisfy a craving for alcohol, as we all know it isn't really too hard to crack open a bottle. However, hear me out. Baking with alcohol is fun and adds a real hit of flavour wherever it's used. Replacing common flavourings like vanilla with a spoonful of coffee liqueur or another strongly flavoured spirit creates really interesting results. You can bake with your favourite tipple, or see it as a creative way of using up bottles of things you'd rather not drink.

Christmas is a time of year I strongly associate with alcohol. Seeing Christmas puddings set alight is a magical moment, and the inevitability of the plate and the tablecloth also going up in flames only increases the drama. Christmas cakes are soaked in brandy, preserving the sponge and giving a boozy hit to each bite. We host a big Christmas Eve party every year, so our table gets stacked with bottles that people bring – everything from mulled wine to tequila. Any leftovers tend to stick around for most of the year, waiting to be used in a baking experiment before the next Christmas comes around.

Alcohols are the product of a craft, made carefully to maximise flavour. Some are best appreciated in their pure form, while others are best shaken into cocktails or paired with flavours which complement them. Everyone loves bakes themed on their favourite drinks, and most recipes that specify one kind of alcohol can easily be substituted with another of a similar strength to keep everyone happy.

Aroma

Unscrew the lid from a bottle of brandy or other strong spirit and the smell hits you immediately. Alcohol molecules are more volatile than water molecules, so they evaporate and deliver aromas to your nose more quickly. Macerating fruits in liquor helps carry the delicate aroma from the fruit, which enhances the eating experience and appreciation of the fruit flavours.

See: Cherry Kirsch Soufflés

Flavour

Alcohol can carry water-soluble flavour compounds that make food taste better, as well as enhance the aroma of foods (see left). A lot of alcohols already possess strong flavours, which add dimensions of sweetness, acidity and richness to bakes. These flavours are determined by the fermentation process, type of grain or fruit and storage method. Alcohols that ferment in wooden barrels, for example, take on woody, smoky notes. Avoid cheap booze – like any ingredient, quality matters, and cheaper varieties of most alcoholic drinks will end up tasting bitter. *See:* Brandy Butter Bread Pudding

Burning off

For years I cooked with alcohol, thinking that most of it evaporated during the cooking process, leaving only the flavour behind. But recently I discovered that, while cooking does reduce the percentage of alcohol in a dish, it does not 'burn off' completely. Different cooking techniques result in varying amounts of alcohol being retained. Showy preparation like flambéing crêpes by igniting spirits in the pan only burns off 25 per cent of the added alcohol but baking alcohol in a sponge will burn off 65 per cent. *See:* Bramble Crêpes Suzette

Soaking

Alcohol-rich syrups brushed over sponges can take your baking to a whole new level. They are fantastic at penetrating into breads like babas, and are easily absorbed by fresh and dried fruits, causing them to swell and become bloated with boozy goodness. *See:* Mai Tai Rum Babas

Tiramisu pots

Using a flavoured alcohol to enhance an ingredient is a clever way of intensifying flavour. Each spoonful of these tiramisu pots has a strong coffee kick with a little background warmth from the liqueur, mellowed with creamy, light mascarpone.

1. Pour the cooled coffee into a small shallow bowl and stir in the coffee liqueur.

2. In a separate bowl, beat the egg and caster sugar together for a few minutes using an electric hand-held whisk until really light and fluffy. The mixture should double in volume.

3. Add the mascarpone and double cream to the whipped eggs and sugar, and whisk again until the mixture has thickened and no lumps of mascarpone remain.

4. Have 4 small glass tumblers or jars ready for assembly. Break 6 of the biscuits in half and dunk each piece in the coffee mixture for 3 seconds. Divide the soaked biscuit halves among the glasses, then spoon a few tablespoons of the cream mixture over the top and dust the top of the cream with some of the cocoa powder, to create layers.

5. Halve and soak the remaining biscuits and repeat the process, layering the glasses until you have used up all the biscuits and mascarpone cream mixture. Smooth the surface and dust the top with the remaining cocoa powder. Enjoy immediately or chill for a few hours to firm up.

SERVES 4
PREP TIME: 10 MINS

150ml cooled strong coffee
50ml coffee liqueur, such as Tia Maria or Kahlúa
1 egg
25g caster sugar
150g mascarpone
150ml double cream
12 Savoiardi or Lady Fingers biscuits
2 tbsp cocoa powder

ALCOHOL

200

Bramble crêpes Suzette

I don't know about you, but I love a pud with a bit of drama. Christmas pudding is always exciting with its flaming top – but why flambé just once a year? This is my take on a retro classic, replacing orange liqueur with blackcurrant crème de cassis and brandy to update it. It's vibrantly coloured, boozy and on fire, so makes for an impressive end to a meal or a naughty breakfast option!

MAKES 4 CRÊPES
PREP TIME: 5 MINS
COOKING TIME: 15 MINS

CRÊPES
75g plain flour
125ml milk
1 egg
1 tbsp butter
Mint leaves, to serve

SAUCE
100g blackberries
50g caster sugar
50g butter
2 tbsp crème de cassis liqueur
1 tbsp brandy (optional)

1. Sift the flour into a large bowl and make a well in the centre. Whisk the milk, 25ml of water and the egg in a jug until well combined, then gradually pour the wet mixture into the flour, whisking all the time. Melt the butter in a large frying pan (which you'll use to fry the crêpes), then add it to the crêpe batter and stir to combine.

2. Heat the frying pan over a medium–high heat. When the pan is hot, spoon a small ladleful of batter into the pan. Swirl to coat the base of the pan, then cook for about 30 seconds or until the pancake is golden on the bottom, then flip over and cook the other side for another 30 seconds. Turn out the cooked crêpe on to a large plate and set to one side. Make 3 more pancakes in the same way.

3. To make the sauce, crush the blackberries in a small bowl using a fork then press them through a sieve, collecting the blackberry juice in the now empty frying pan. Add the sugar and butter to the pan and simmer over a medium heat, stirring until the butter has melted. Allow the sauce to bubble for 2–3 minutes or until it has thickened and become syrup-like, then stir in the crème de cassis.

4. Fold each crêpe into quarters and arrange them in the sauce. Heat over a medium heat for a few minutes until the sauce is bubbling, then flip the quartered crêpes over to warm through.

5. If you wish, flambé the crêpes by heating the brandy gently in a small saucepan. Set light to the warmed brandy in the pan and immediately pour it over the crêpes in the frying pan. Serve the crêpes with a sprinkle of torn mint leaves as soon as the flames die down.

Amaretto syllabubs

This quick dish is ideal to whip up when you forget to make dessert. It's definitely not for the faint-hearted as the Amaretto is strong, but it's a big hit of flavour in a light, refreshing mouthful which makes it perfect after a heavy dinner. The lemon juice helps thicken the cream, as well as lifting the syllabub with citrus notes. Creating the chocolate pattern on the inside of the glass is one of my favourite secret tricks for making a simple dessert look spectacular, and it only takes seconds to achieve. A ten-minute show-off dessert at its finest!

1. Melt the chocolate in a heatproof bowl set over a pan of simmering water or in the microwave and spoon into a piping bag. Allow to cool for a few minutes, then cut off the tip of the bag and swirl a pattern of chocolate over the insides of 4 wide-rimmed stem glasses and place in the fridge to set.

2. Combine the caster sugar, amaretto and lemon juice in a large bowl and stir until the grains of sugar dissolve. Pour in the cream and whisk the mixture by hand until it thickens and soft peaks are just beginning to form. Try not to over-whip the dessert or it won't have a silky, light texture.

3. Spoon the syllabub into the chilled chocolate-swirled glasses and serve immediately or chill until ready to eat. Serve with a few amaretti biscuits on the side or crushed over the top.

SERVES 4
PREP TIME: 10 MINS

50g dark chocolate, chopped
50g caster sugar
100ml amaretto liqueur
Juice of ½ lemon
300ml double cream
Amaretti biscuits (shop-bought or see page 74), to serve

You will also need a disposable piping bag.

Brandy butter bread pudding

I'm not ashamed to admit that I love food shopping, especially when supermarkets start filling their shelves with Christmas treats. Brandy butter is one of my favourite arrivals; I could eat it by the spoonful. If it's the wrong time of year to find brandy butter on the shelves, simply make your own by beating together equal amounts of butter and icing sugar, and adding brandy to taste.

SERVES 8

PREP TIME: 15 MINS

COOKING TIME: 25–30 MINS

Unsalted butter, for greasing
300ml whole milk
300ml double cream
1 vanilla pod, seeds scraped out
4 eggs
50g caster sugar
2 tbsp brandy
250g brioche loaf, cut into 1.5cm slices
100g brandy butter
1 tbsp demerara sugar

You will also need a 1.5 litre baking dish.

1. Preheat the oven to 180°C/160°C fan/gas 4 and grease the baking dish with butter.

2. Place the milk, cream, vanilla pod and vanilla seeds in a small saucepan and heat over a medium heat until steaming. While the mixture is heating up, whisk together the eggs and sugar in a large heatproof jug until smooth.

3. Remove the vanilla pod from the milk and cream, and pour the hot mixture into the eggs and sugar very slowly, whisking all the time. Whisk in the brandy and set to one side.

4. Butter both sides of each brioche slice liberally with the brandy butter.

5. Arrange the buttered brioche slices in the greased dish, overlapping them at the edges. Pour over the custard mixture, making sure it covers all the exposed bread. Sprinkle over the demerara sugar, then bake the pudding for 25–30 minutes until the top is golden brown and the custard has set. Remove from the oven and serve immediately.

Whiskey rye chocolate chip cookies

Whiskey is often made using rye grain, so using rye flour in these cookies takes them right back to their humble beginnings and brings out their nutty, slightly spicy flavour. Adding alcohol to the cookie dough stops the biscuits from becoming too tough as it limits gluten formation. This gives these biscuits a great 'melt-in-the-mouth' quality as well as a fantastic whiskey flavour. Make sure you chill the dough so the flavours can infuse and the butter solidify, as this is really important for thick, chewy cookies!

1. Beat the butter with both the sugars in a large bowl using a wooden spoon until they are well combined (there is no need for it to be light and fluffy).

2. Add the egg to the butter mixture and beat again, then stir in the whiskey until the mixture is smooth.

3. Combine the plain flour, rye flour, bicarbonate of soda and baking powder in a bowl. Tip the dry ingredients into the wet mixture and fold together using a spatula until a stiff dough forms. Stir through the chocolate chunks. Transfer the bowl of dough to the fridge to chill for at least 30 minutes.

4. Preheat the oven to 180°C/160°C fan/gas 4 and grease and line 2 large baking sheets with baking parchment or silicone baking sheets.

5. Use an ice-cream scoop to form 12 balls of dough (a tablespoon will work too, but the cookies won't be as regularly shaped) and place them on the sheets, leaving enough space for them to spread out. Try not to roll the balls of dough, as the ragged top created by the scoop or tablespoon will give the cookies the traditional cracked surface.

6. Bake the cookies for 12–15 minutes or until the mixture has spread out and browned around the edges. They will look undercooked and puffy in the centre, but this will settle and firm up into a chewy, soft centre. Remove from the oven and allow to cool for at least 10 minutes on the sheets.

MAKES 12 LARGE COOKIES

PREP TIME: 15 MINS PLUS CHILLING

COOKING TIME: 12–15 MINS

150g butter, softened, plus extra for greasing
125g soft light brown sugar
100g caster sugar
1 large egg
2 tbsp whiskey
150g strong plain flour
100g rye flour
½ tsp bicarbonate of soda
½ tsp baking powder
100g dark chocolate, chopped

Bourbon biscuits

When offered a plate of biscuits as a child, a good old chocolate Bourbon was always my biscuit of choice. There was a ritual in eating them too; pulling them apart and licking off the icing first was the biscuit etiquette. As an adult, I've often wondered why Bourbon biscuits don't actually contain bourbon, so I've spiked them and the buttercream with a big glug of whiskey. Good bourbon has notes of caramel and warming spices like cinnamon, which pairs perfectly with dark chocolate.

1. Cream the butter and sugar together in a bowl with a wooden spoon or an electric hand-held whisk for 1–2 minutes until pale and fluffy. Beat in the honey until the mixture is smooth.

2. Combine the flour, cocoa powder and bicarbonate of soda in a small bowl then sift it over the butter and sugar mixture. Stir until the mixture clumps together, then add the whiskey and beat again until a dough forms. Tip the dough on to a sheet of cling film and knead briefly, then wrap it in the cling film and chill it for 20 minutes so the butter can solidify.

3. Preheat the oven to 180°C/160°C fan/gas 4 and line 2 baking sheets with baking parchment. Unwrap the chilled dough and roll it out on a lightly floured worktop or between 2 pieces of cling film to a thickness of about 5mm. Use a sharp knife to cut out about 50 rectangles (3 x 7cm) or use a crimped cutter if you have one, and arrange them on the baking sheets. Mark a series of holes over the top of each biscuit using a skewer, or stamp them with letters.

4. Bake the biscuits for 10–12 minutes until slightly puffy and crisp, then remove and allow to cool on the sheets for 5 minutes. Transfer the biscuits to a wire rack to cool completely.

5. Make the bourbon buttercream by beating the butter and icing sugar together using an electric hand-held whisk until really light and fluffy. Add the cocoa powder and whiskey, then beat again until smooth. Add a little more whiskey to taste, if desired. Pipe or spread the buttercream on to half the biscuits and sandwich with the other halves.

MAKES ABOUT 25 BISCUITS

PREP TIME: 15 MINS PLUS CHILLING

COOKING TIME: 10–12 MINS

125g butter, softened
125g caster sugar
2 tbsp runny honey
250g plain flour, plus extra for dusting
50g cocoa powder
1 tsp bicarbonate of soda
3 tbsp bourbon whiskey

BUTTERCREAM FILLING
100g unsalted butter, softened
200g icing sugar
1 tbsp cocoa powder
3 tbsp bourbon whiskey, plus extra to taste (optional)

Cherry kirsch soufflés

When I made my first soufflé, I felt I'd reached new heights in baking. Fancy, French and glamorous – I was almost disappointed to find out that they aren't as difficult to make as their reputation suggests. If you can make a custard, and you can make a meringue, you can make an impressive little soufflé. Add some dark chocolate and kirsch-soaked cherries into the mix and you are on to a winner.

MAKES 4 SOUFFLÉS

PREP TIME: 20 MINS

**COOKING TIME:
14–16 MINS**

Butter, for greasing
100g pitted cherries, halved
2 tbsp kirsch
2 eggs, separated
45g caster sugar, plus 1 tsp extra for coating
1 tbsp cocoa powder
25g cornflour
150ml whole milk
75g dark chocolate, chopped
25g butter, cubed

1. Preheat the oven to 200°C/180°C fan/gas 6. Grease 4 small ramekins liberally with butter, then sprinkle ½ teaspoon of the extra sugar into each one and tilt them to coat the edges as well as the base with sugar. Place the ramekins on a baking tray.

2. Put the halved cherries in a small bowl and pour over the kirsch. Leave the cherries to soak in the alcohol while you make the soufflé mixture.

3. Put the egg whites in a small clean grease-free bowl and whisk with an electric hand-held whisk or by hand until soft peaks form. Add 2 tablespoons of the sugar and whisk again until stiff, glossy peaks form. Set to one side.

4. Place the egg yolks, remaining sugar, cocoa powder and cornflour in a large jug and whisk (no need to clean the beaters) until combined and slightly paler in colour.

5. Pour the milk into a saucepan and heat over a medium heat until steaming. Gradually pour the hot milk into the egg yolk mixture, whisking all the time until the mixture is smooth.

6. Transfer the custard mixture back into the saucepan and heat gently for a few minutes, stirring all the time with a spatula, until the custard is thick and smooth. Remove from the heat and stir in the chopped chocolate and the butter. When both the chocolate and butter have melted and no lumps remain, pour the mixture into a bowl and allow to cool for a few minutes.

7. When the chocolate custard mixture is cool enough to touch comfortably, fold in a spoonful of the egg white mixture to loosen it slightly. Gently fold in the remaining egg whites, being careful not to knock out too much air. Stop folding as soon as you can no longer see large lumps of egg white.

8. Divide the soaked cherries and any remaining liquid among the ramekins and top with the soufflé mixture. Bake for 14–16 minutes until risen, with a slight wobble in the centre. Serve immediately.

Pisco sour angel food cake

Angel food cake is fatless, which gives it a unique spongy texture that is ideal for soaking up lots of lovely syrup; especially when it's alcoholic! I was introduced to Pisco Sours in a Peruvian restaurant in Marylebone, London, and I knew they had to be transformed into a cake. The white grape brandy is paired with tangy lime juice, sugar syrup and egg whites to make the cocktail, and you'll find all those elements in this cake.

1. Preheat the oven to 180°C/160°C fan/gas 4. You do not need to grease the tin as the cake needs the friction with the tin to rise.

2. Beat the egg whites and cream of tartar in a large bowl with an electric hand-held whisk until they form soft peaks. The whites should hold their shape, but not be stiff enough to turn upside down over your head, like when making meringue.

3. Sift the flour and icing sugar together into a small bowl. Carefully fold the dry mixture into the whisked egg whites, a few tablespoons at a time, using a flexible spatula. Keep as much air in the mixture as possible, folding only until the flour has just disappeared. Stir in the lime zest and gently spoon the mixture into the tin. Bake in the centre of the oven for 30–35 minutes or until the sponge is golden brown and a skewer inserted into its centre comes out clean.

4. Remove from the oven and immediately flip the tin upside down on to a wire rack. Leave the cake to cool upside down in the tin (this stops the cake from collapsing as it cools). When cool, run a palette knife around the inside of the tin to release the cake.

5. While the cake is cooling, make the soaking syrup by combining the caster sugar, 50ml of water and the lime juice in a small saucepan. Simmer over a medium heat for 1 minute until the sugar dissolves, then remove from the heat, stir in the pisco and allow to cool.

6. Whip the cream for the topping into soft peaks. Use a serrated knife to slice the cake into three layers of equal thickness. Brush each layer of the cake with the syrup, making sure it is well soaked for maximum flavour.

7. Stack the soaked sponge layers on a cake stand, spreading a thin layer of whipped cream between each one. Cover the top and sides of the cake with the remaining cream, sprinkle with the lime zest and serve immediately.

SERVES 8–10

PREP TIME: 20 MINS
PLUS COOLING

COOKING TIME:
30–35 MINS

ANGEL FOOD CAKE
8 large egg whites
1 tsp cream of tartar
175g plain flour
175g icing sugar
Grated zest of 1 unwaxed lime

SOAKING SYRUP
100g caster sugar
Juice of 2 limes
50ml pisco (grape brandy)

TOPPING
250ml double cream
Grated zest of 1 unwaxed lime, to sprinkle

You will also need a 25cm angel food cake tin and a cake stand.

Mai Tai rum babas

I'm not sure whose job it is to consign recipes to the 'passé' folder, but the baba certainly shouldn't be there! There is nothing not to like about puffy yeasted buns saturated in rum syrup, especially when it's inspired by the Mai Tai cocktail. Mai Tai is Tahitian for 'good', and it definitely lives up to that description, combining two types of rum with zesty orange and lime. It's a tiki flavour sensation that gives the dated baba a new meaning.

1. Grease the savarin moulds or 8 holes of the muffin tin with oil and set to one side.

2. Pour the milk into a small saucepan and add the butter. Heat gently over a low heat until the butter has melted, then remove from the heat and allow to cool to room temperature.

3. Place the flour in a large mixing bowl or the bowl of a stand mixer and add the sugar and yeast to one side and the salt to the other. Make a well in the centre and pour in the lukewarm milk and butter and the beaten eggs. Stir until a soft, sticky dough forms then beat in the orange and lime zest.

4. Knead the dough in the bowl for 10 minutes until it is smooth and elastic. Alternatively, knead the dough using a stand mixer fitted with the dough-hook attachment for 5 minutes. Cover the bowl with cling film or a damp tea towel and leave the dough to rise at room temperature for 1–3 hours until doubled in size.

5. When the dough has risen, knock it back in the bowl and divide it into 4 equal sausage shapes or 8 round pieces (depending on which tins you are using). Place the dough in the tins and cover with oiled cling film, then leave to rise at room temperature for 1 hour or until the dough has risen above the top of the tins.

6. Preheat the oven to 200°C/180°C fan/gas 6. Bake the babas for 20 minutes if using savarin moulds, or 15 minutes if you have used a muffin tin, until golden brown all over.

7. While the babas are cooking, make the soaking syrup. Place the caster sugar in a saucepan and pour in the orange and lime juices. Heat over a low heat, stirring all the time, until the sugar has dissolved, then turn up the heat and simmer for 2 minutes until the mixture has thickened slightly. Remove from the heat and stir in the rum.

MAKES 4 LARGE RUM BABAS OR 8 SMALL BABAS

PREP TIME: 30 MINS PLUS PROVING

COOKING TIME: 15–20 MINS

BABA
Oil, for greasing
75ml whole milk
100g butter, cubed
225g plain flour
25g caster sugar
1 x 7g sachet fast-action dried yeast
½ tsp table salt
2 eggs, beaten
Grated zest of 1 large unwaxed orange
Grated zest of 2 unwaxed limes

SOAKING SYRUP
300g caster sugar
Juice of 1 large orange
Juice of 2 limes
200ml dark rum
100ml white rum
200ml double cream, to serve
Grated unwaxed lime zest, to serve

You will also need 4 x 10cm savarin moulds or a 12-hole muffin tin and a disposable piping bag.

ALCOHOL

210

8. When the babas are cooked, remove them from the oven and allow to cool for 10 minutes then remove from the tins. Pour a small amount of syrup into the bottom of the empty tins, then return the babas to the tins to soak up the syrup. Spoon some of the remaining syrup over the babas and leave to cool.

9. When you are ready to serve, turn the babas out on to plates and drizzle over the remaining syrup. Whip the cream into soft peaks and pipe it on to the top of the babas then sprinkle them with lime zest.

Espresso Martini cheesecake

An espresso Martini is an indulgent cocktail made up of vodka, coffee liqueur and espresso. It's creamy and rich, so naturally lends itself to cheesecake form! The soured-cream layer on the top is often found on a New York cheesecake and complements the coffee flavour really well to create the recognisable white top of an espresso Martini.

SERVES 10–12

PREP TIME: 20 MINS PLUS CHILLING

COOKING TIME: 1 HOUR–1 HOUR 10 MINS

BASE
50g butter, plus extra for greasing
200g digestive biscuits
1 tbsp cocoa powder

CHEESECAKE
600g soft full-fat cream cheese
150g caster sugar
2 tbsp cornflour
2 tbsp instant espresso powder
2 eggs, beaten
100ml double cream
75ml Kahlúa or other coffee liqueur
50ml vodka

TOPPING
250ml soured cream
1 tbsp caster sugar
Chocolate-coated coffee beans

You will also need a 20cm-round loose-bottomed cake tin.

1. Grease the cake tin and line it with baking parchment. Melt the butter in a small saucepan or microwave. Blitz the digestive biscuits in a food processor with the cocoa powder until they resemble fine crumbs, then pour the melted butter into the processor and blitz again. Alternatively, place the biscuits and cocoa powder in a plastic bag, seal and crush with a rolling pin. Press the crumbs into the base of the lined tin, pushing them right into the edges with the back of a spoon to get an even layer. Place the base in the fridge to chill.

2. Preheat the oven to 170°C/150°C fan/gas 3. Beat the cream cheese and sugar together in a large bowl until smooth, then stir in the cornflour and espresso powder.

3. Add the eggs and stir gently, trying not to incorporate too much air, then mix in the double cream, Kahlúa and vodka.

4. Remove the base from the fridge and wrap the bottom of the tin in a double layer of tin foil so the cheesecake mixture doesn't leak out. Place the cake tin in a roasting tin and boil a kettle.

5. Pour the cheesecake mixture into the chilled base. Fill the roasting tin with boiling water until it reaches halfway up the cheesecake tin. Bake the cheesecake for 50 minutes–1 hour or until the top feels set with a slight wobble in the centre. Remove the cheesecake from the oven and allow to cool for 10 minutes (still in the roasting tin of water).

6. To make the topping, beat the soured cream with the caster sugar and carefully spread it over the top of the cheesecake, being careful not to pierce the surface. Bake for a further 10 minutes then lift the tin out of the water and allow the cheesecake to cool completely at room temperature. Remove the tin foil and chill in the fridge for at least 3 hours or overnight.

7. When you're ready to serve, top the cheesecake with a few chocolate-coated coffee beans.

Mulled wine pavlova

Love it or hate it, there is no denying that mulled wine symbolises the start of the Christmas period. My family are often given bottles of the stuff at Christmas, and if you're not going to drink it all it is perfect for poaching fruit. Use any fruits you like – I love the combination of pears, plums and cherries in the richly spiced syrup. The size of the fruit dictates for how long it needs to be poached, so make sure to start with large, harder fruits and finish with small, softer ones. Build the pavlova as tall as you can so the fruit can be displayed on top in a generous pile! I heat the sugar before preparing my meringue as it makes the pavlova more stable, but if you're in a rush you can skip this step (though this makes it more likely to crack when baked).

1. Start by making the meringue. Preheat the oven to 220°C/200°C fan/gas 7 and line a large baking tray with baking parchment.

2. Pour the sugar for the meringue on to the lined baking tray and spread it out in an even layer. Warm it in the oven for 5–6 minutes or until the sugar feels hot to the touch and the very edges of the sugar are just starting to melt.

3. While the sugar is heating up, place the egg whites in a large clean, grease-free bowl or bowl of a stand mixer. Whisk the egg whites using an electric hand-held whisk or stand mixer until they form stiff peaks.

4. Carefully whisk the hot sugar into the egg whites, adding a spoonful at a time and letting each spoonful be fully incorporated before adding the next. Avoid adding any of the melted sugar around the edges of the baking tray – this will not dissolve properly.

5. When all the sugar has been added, turn the mixer speed up and whisk for 8–10 minutes or until the mixture is really thick and glossy. If you rub a small amount between your fingers, you shouldn't be able to feel any grains of sugar. If it still feels gritty, continue to whisk for a few more minutes until it feels smooth.

SERVES 8–10

PREP TIME: 40 MINS PLUS COOLING

COOKING TIME: 2–2¼ HOURS

MERINGUE
360g caster sugar
6 egg whites, at room temperature

POACHED FRUIT TOPPING
450ml mulled wine
1 cinnamon stick
4 cloves
100g caster sugar
Grated zest and juice of 1 unwaxed orange
2 pears, peeled, cored and sliced
2 red plums, stoned and quartered
100g cherries, halved and pitted
350ml double cream, to serve

6. Turn the oven down to 120°C/100°C fan/gas ½ and line a baking sheet with a clean sheet of parchment. Spoon the meringue on to the sheet, piling it up to create a tall mound. Bake the pavlova for 2–2¼ hours, then turn the oven off and allow the pavlova to cool completely in the oven (this will take about 1 hour).

7. While the pavlova is baking, make the poached fruit topping. Combine the mulled wine, cinnamon, cloves, caster sugar and orange juice and zest in a saucepan and heat over a low heat, stirring until the sugar has dissolved. Bring the mixture to a gentle simmer, then add the pear pieces. Cook for 15 minutes until the pear pieces are tender, then add the plums and poach for a further 5 minutes. Add the cherries for the last minute of the poaching time.

8. Remove the fruit using a slotted spoon and place it in a bowl to cool. Continue to simmer the poaching liquid until it has reduced by two-thirds and is thick and syrupy, then pour it into a heatproof jug and allow to cool.

9. When you're ready to assemble the pavlova, whip the cream in a bowl until it forms soft peaks and spoon it on to the cool pavlova. Top with a pile of cooled poached fruit, then drizzle liberally with the poaching syrup before serving immediately.

EXPRESS

You can make smaller meringue nests to top with the poached fruit for a more sophisticated individual portion. Make the meringue up to step 5, then pipe or spoon 6–8 small nests, creating an indent in the middle for the fruit to sit. Bake for 1–1 ¼ hours at 120°C/100°C fan/gas ½ before allowing to cool completely in the oven. Finish in the same way as above.

Irish Cream pretzel cake

This is a really fun cake, combining a favourite late-night tipple with a bar snack you'd enjoy with it. Covering the outside of the cake with pretzels is simple but creates an impressive-looking cake, and the gentle saltiness cuts through the richness of the Baileys and the coffee perfectly. Here's a unique cake that everyone will love!

1. Preheat the oven to 180°C/160°C fan/gas 4; grease the cake tins and line them with baking parchment.

2. Cream the butter and sugar together in a bowl, using a stand mixer fitted with the paddle attachment or an electric hand-held whisk, until pale and fluffy. Beat in the eggs, one at a time, adding 1–2 tablespoons of the flour if the mixture curdles.

3. In a separate bowl, combine the flour and baking powder. Gradually add the dry mixture to the butter and egg mixture, followed by the coffee and the Baileys, until a thick batter forms.

4. Divide the mixture evenly among the tins and use a spatula to smooth the tops. Bake for 20–25 minutes or until the cakes are firm to the touch and a skewer inserted into the centre of each cake comes out clean. Remove from the oven and allow the cakes to cool for 10 minutes in the tin, then transfer to a wire rack to cool completely.

5. To make the ganache, place the butter and chocolate in a heatproof bowl over a pan of simmering water. Stir until the mixture is melted and smooth. Remove from the heat and pour in the double cream and the Baileys, then mix until combined. Place in the fridge and chill for 30 minutes until cool but not set firm.

6. Whip the cooled ganache with an electric hand-held whisk for 2–3 minutes until it turns from dark to pale brown. Use a spatula to scrape down the sides of the bowl to make sure all the ganache is properly whipped.

7. When the sponges are completely cool, assemble the cake. Put a small blob of the ganache on a cake stand or serving plate (use a cake turntable if you have one) and place the first layer of sponge on top of it. Spread the first layer of sponge with quarter of the ganache using a palette knife, then top with the second layer of sponge. Repeat the process, then cover the whole cake with the remaining ganache. Run the palette knife around the outside of the cake to smooth it over and create a swirl on the top. Push the pretzels into the outside of the cake until the whole cake is covered, allowing them to peek over the top of the cake.

SERVES 12

PREP TIME: 30 MINS PLUS COOLING

COOKING TIME: 20–25 MINS

SPONGE
225g butter, softened, plus extra for greasing
225g soft light brown sugar
4 eggs, at room temperature
225g plain flour
3 tsp baking powder
2 tbsp instant coffee granules, dissolved in 1 tbsp boiling water
2 tbsp Baileys Irish Cream Liqueur

BAILEYS GANACHE
150g salted butter, cubed
300g dark chocolate, chopped
200ml double cream
100ml Baileys Irish Cream Liqueur

TO DECORATE
175g bag pretzels

You will also need 3 x 18cm-round cake tins.

Gin and tonic lime pie

What has Key lime pie always needed? Gin! This recipe uses tonic-water syrup to make the Italian meringue topping so that the essence of G&T is in every mouthful. Gin has a clean, perfumed flavour that matches brilliantly with lime, and the bitterness from quinine in the sweet meringue makes for a perfectly balanced pie.

1. Preheat the oven to 200°C/180°C fan/gas 6.

2. To make the base, melt the butter in the microwave or in a small saucepan. Place the digestive biscuits in a small food processor and blitz to a powder, then pour in the melted butter and blitz again until all the crumbs are coated in butter. Alternatively, place the biscuits in a plastic bag and use a rolling pin to crush them to a fine powder, then put the crumbs in a bowl and stir in the butter until the crumbs are completely coated.

3. Press the crumbs into the tart tin, making sure they cover the bottom and sides in an even layer. Use the back of a spoon to press them down firmly. Bake the crust in the oven for 10 minutes while you make the filling.

4. Pour the condensed milk into a large bowl and add the egg yolks, lime juice and zest. Whisk together with a balloon whisk, then add the gin and beat again.

5. Turn the oven down to 180°C/160°C fan/gas 4. Pour the filling into the crust and bake for 10–15 minutes until the filling is set with a slight wobble in the centre. Remove from the oven and chill for at least 30 minutes.

6. When you're nearly ready to serve, make the Italian tonic-water meringue topping. Put the sugar and tonic water in a small saucepan and warm over a low heat, stirring until the sugar has dissolved and the mixture turns from cloudy to clear. Turn the heat up to high. Allow the syrup to boil without stirring until it reaches 118°C on the sugar thermometer.

7. While the syrup is coming up to temperature, whisk the egg whites in the clean, grease-free bowl of a stand mixer or using an electric hand-held whisk until they form soft peaks when you lift the beaters out. As soon as the syrup is hot enough, take it off the heat and pour it gradually in the egg whites, beating all the time. (Pour the syrup down the side of the bowl rather than directly on to the beaters.) Once all the syrup has been added, continue to whisk on high speed for a further 5 minutes until the mixture is glossy and stiff.

8. Spoon the meringue on to the top of the pie and use a blowtorch to gently brown it. You could also place the pie under the grill, watching carefully so it doesn't burn. Serve with a glass of chilled G&T for a summery treat.

SERVES 8–10

PREP TIME: 20 MINS PLUS CHILLING

COOKING TIME: 20–25 MINS

BASE
100g butter
200g digestive biscuits

FILLING
1 x 397g tin condensed milk
4 egg yolks (use the whites in the meringue below)
Grated zest and juice of 4 unwaxed limes
3 tbsp gin

ITALIAN MERINGUE TOPPING
200g caster sugar
150ml tonic water
4 egg whites

You will also need a 23cm loose-bottomed springform tart tin and a sugar thermometer.

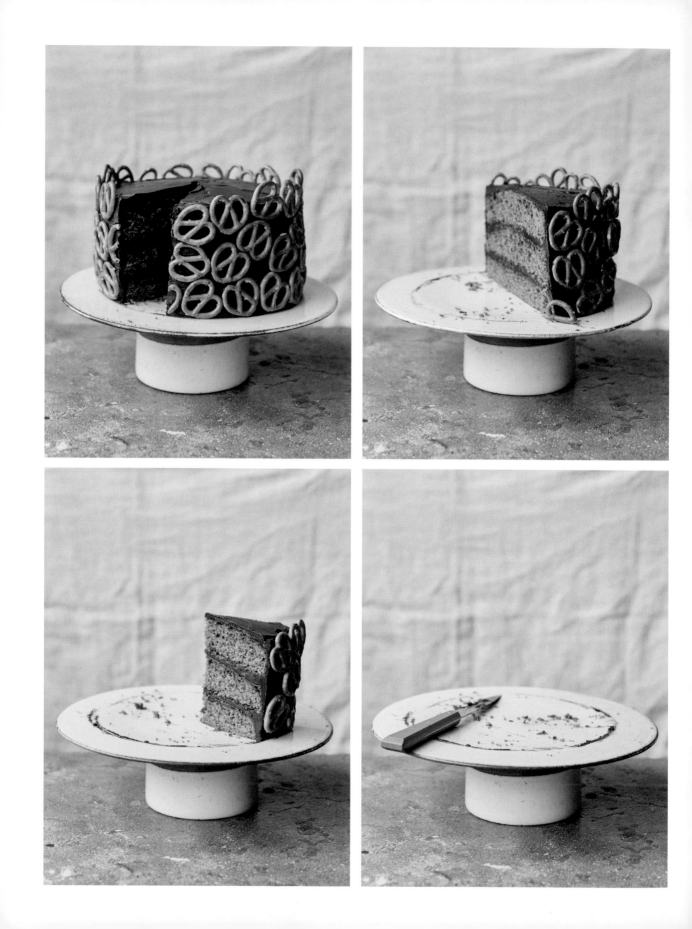

Index

Acknowledgements

This is my favourite page in the book to write, as writing a book involves quite a crowd of wonderful people who deserve more recognition than I could possibly do justice with a few sentences.

Firstly, thanks to Grace Cheetham and the team at HarperCollins for making this book happen! I couldn't (and still can hardly!) believe that I have had the opportunity to write a second book, and I am so grateful. You understood exactly what I wanted this book to be as soon as we spoke, and I am so honoured to write for you.

To my fabulous shoot team: thank you for making everything look so beautiful and delicious! Laura Edwards – your snapping skills have bought this book to life and you make your work look so effortless. Annie Rigg – the greatest food stylist around and crafter of the best bacon sandwiches. I have learnt so much from you both and it's been a pleasure to work with you.

Sarah Hammond and Simeon Greenaway, you have been so brilliant to work alongside. Thank you for your patience, hard work and fantastic editing and design skills. I am so thrilled with how this book has come together. Thanks also to Polly Webb-Wilson for the stunning props that feature in every single photo, and to Laura, Lola and Kendal for all your help both in the kitchen and studio. Thank you to Debbie Powell for the wonderful illustrations.

Isabel Prodger and Katie Moss, marketing and publicity extraordinaires (and hand models). You made the publicity tours an unbelievable amount of fun with your relentless positivity and excitement.

Claudia Young, my fabulous agent, thank you for everything you do for me. You are second-to-none, know my life inside out and helped the idea for this book turn into reality – something of which I am so grateful. Thanks for all the encouragement.

To my family: Mum, Dad and Han. You've done it again. You thought that enduring hundreds of bake tests and the days of a constantly messy kitchen were over and then I subjected you to another year of chaos. Thank you for being so gracious, keeping me grounded and supporting me so wonderfully, I really couldn't have written this without you.

Wendy, Jo, Fin, Grandma, Jona and Clare; your help and feedback has been invaluable. I hope you can flick through this book and know that you played a big part in its creation.

To Michael, the man who claims half the ideas in this book are his own and makes me laugh too much when I'm trying to focus on writing. You've stood by my side even when we are miles apart and pushed me to keep going when I've felt like I couldn't. Love you!

'Taste and see that the Lord is good; blessed is the one who takes refuge in him.'

Psalm 34:8